ROMANCING THE
King

ROMANCING THE *King*

FINDING INTIMACY WITH GOD

BRIAN LAKE

DESTINY IMAGE® PUBLISHERS, INC.
PO Box 310, Shippensburg, PA 17257-0310

"Speaking to the Purposes of God for This Generation and for the Generations to Come."

This book and all other Destiny Image, Revival Press, MercyPlace, Fresh Bread, Destiny Image Fiction, and Treasure House books are available at Christian bookstores and distributors worldwide.

Previously published by STM Publications copyright 2008 as *Romancing the King: A Divine Romance Between God and Ma*n
ISBN 978-0-9780000-0-0

For a U.S. bookstore nearest you, call 1-800-722-6774.
For more information on foreign distributors, call 717-532-3040.
Reach us on the Internet: www.destinyimage.com.

Trade Paper ISBN 13: 978-0-7684-3268-8
Hardcover ISBN 978-0-7684-3491-0
Large Print ISBN 978-0-7684-3492-7
E-book ISBN 978-0-7684-9097-8

For Worldwide Distribution, Printed in the U.S.A.
2 3 4 5 6 7 / 19 18 17 16 15

I dedicate this book to my King Jesus, who saved and called me into His kingdom. It will always be about You! My life and everything I have is because of You. I am eternally grateful.

To my wife, Pamela, who is my best friend; for her support while writing this book and for her daily encouragement and joy in life and ministry.

To my children, Jordon, Molly, and Melanie, who make me a proud father.

To my parents, Donald and Marna Lake, for their tremendous support and love. Thanks for being great parents!

To my uncle, David "Mack" McQuade, for introducing me to God when I was a young boy. We had many wonderful memories together. I will never forget what you have done for me.

To my pastors, Bill and Ann Chilcote, for their mentorship, friendship, and encouragement. I am honored and privileged to have pastors like you.

To my spiritual foundation mentor in Christ, Kenneth Copeland, who has been a great source of support and inspiration for the Kingdom of God.

To my friends Jill Austin, Paul Moore, and Lynne Whelan, who encouraged me or helped this manuscript become a reality.

Endorsements

As we get closer to the return of Messiah, this earth will shake. The only people who will stand will be those who have achieved intimacy with the King. Watch the increase of miracles as you follow the revelation from the Book of Esther for _Romancing the King_.

Sid Roth,
Host, "It's Supernatural!" Television
www.SidRoth.org

Brian Lake not only has a pure spirit and sincere faith, he has discovered the secret of vibrant life in the Kingdom. Discover the secret as you read _Romancing the King_.

Patricia King
Founder, Extreme Prophetic
Extreme Prophetic TV
Author, _Spiritual Revolution_

Romancing the King is a clear call to divine intimacy with the living God. Brian's desire to see a generation return to radical love for Christ is refreshing. I recommend you read this book over and over again! It will encourage and change your life!

Bobby Conner
Founder, Eagle's View Ministries
Author, *God's Supernatural Power*

Brian Lake's ministry is filled with spectacular miracles and changed lives, but instead of writing about his ministry, he writes about his secret: friendship with God. Brian spends time re-evaluating Scriptures that have become too familiar to us, highlighting how it is all about the heart. I was stirred by Brian's efforts, and you will be too.

Shawn Bolz
Senior Pastor, Expression58
Author, *Keys to Heaven's Economy*
and *The Throne Room Company*

Brian's material fits perfectly with my life's experience. The pages seemed to leap into my spirit with each word. In fact, while reading *Romancing the King*, something profound happened to me. I experienced unity with the author's teaching and then recognized how the Holy Spirit flowed through Brian's writing. The author needs to be congratulated on his ability to yield to God's voice, sharing his personal thoughts and his gentle approach. The Kingdom of God will benefit from this book and so will you!

Pastors Larry and BB Rail
Living Stones Fellowship
Refocus Ministries International

In this hour, God is releasing a greater revelation to obtain an intimate relationship with Him. From Genesis to Revelation, God has been seeking a people who will love Him above everything else. He has always desired intimacy with His people.

In Ephesians 5:31-32, Paul compares the union of a man and a woman to Christ and the Church. It is a mystery how God and humankind can become one, but this is the inheritance available to all believers who will lay down their lives for this great King. The Lord is longing for a people who perfectly reflect His character and nature on the earth as His ambassadors.

In *Romancing the King,* Brian Lake will take you on a journey of intimacy. He pulls from his own personal relationship with God and shares the keys to loving God more. Brian does not just talk about this subject—he lives it. I wholeheartedly recommend this book to you; it will draw you into a divine romance with the King of kings.

Andre Ashby
Founder, Souls Cry Ministries

I am very proud of Brian Lake being first fruits of Fresh Fire's internship program. He has put forth his heart into this book. You will be mightily blessed and encouraged by reading *Romancing the King.* Get ready to gain a full understanding of the King's promise and the King's desire to personally fellowship with you.

David and Darcia Bentley
Founders, Freedom Fire Ministries

Contents

HOLLYWOOD HAS BUILT ITS EMPIRE on the whole concept, notion, and universal theme of "romance." While the movie titles and the scripts change regarding the many love stories that have become box office hits since the earliest days of the silver screen, the theme is forever the same. Love is something the heart longs for; and when love is found and experienced, the shared bliss a couple experiences meets a need that nothing else can. Everyone longs for romance—we were *built* for romance.

The Grand Designer of Creation is the Author of romance. John the Beloved tells us that God is love. The only reason we experience the kind of yearnings we experience for romance is because we are made in the image and likeness of the Great Romancer Himself. It is because of this that there is within the heart of God a desire for deep and profound intimacy with His sons and daughters. While the love between a man and a woman touches a degree of what romance is all about, the ultimate romance is the Divine romance. That is the romance between the deep in our human spirit that calls to the deep in God's Spirit.

The Song of Solomon, which is part of the canon of Scripture, was once thought to be something that had no place in Holy Writ. It unashamedly talks about romance and the exchange of deep intimacy between a Shulamite maiden and a Shepherd-King. Thankfully, it is recognized as divinely inspired. Ultimately, the book isn't about an earthly romance, it is the prophetic picture of the ultimate romance, the romance between the Bridegroom and the Bride. She cries out, *"Let Him kiss me with the kisses of His mouth,"* and asks to be drawn to the Shepherd-King so that they might run together (See Song of Sol. 1:2,4).

How desperately does the King of kings desire intimacy with His Bride, His Beloved. Saint James tells us that *"...the Spirit God has placed within us tends toward jealousy"* (see James 4:5). Yes, God is a jealous Lover and doesn't want His sons and daughters to violate His love and intimacy with them.

We live in a day where a fresh cry is rising in an emerging generation for a deeper sense of abiding with Christ, a deeper sense of union with the Father, a deeper sense of communion in the Holy Spirit. All of this is tied to God's intention for intimacy with us. In this landmark book *Romancing the King*, Brian Lake has taken a bold step in seeking to remind, reclaim, and recover the Lord's testimony regarding the passionate pursuit of His presence in this generation.

The only thing that moves my heart more than dialogue about God's manifest presence is the pursuit and experience of His glorious presence. My heart, in these days, is to live the "presence-driven" lifestyle and to walk with others of like precious faith. Brian Lake is a presence-driven believer and leader in the Kingdom who takes us step by step from the beginning of creation to the culmination of the Kingdom in regard to God's ultimate intention for intimacy, fellowship, and union with Him.

I urge you to take your time as you read each line; and as you read, when the Spirit opens your eyes in glad surprise to the intimacy that is your birthright, stop and pause and worship Him. Acknowledge His presence, and then keep on reading. This is not merely a treatise; this is a manual with keys for transformation.

I am grateful to Brian for his willingness to share both the Father's heart and his heart in this tremendous work. Drink deeply oh lovers!

Dr. Mark J. Chironna
Mark Chironna Ministries
Orlando, Florida

GOD IS UNRELENTING IN PURSUING us and touching our hearts, but what are we doing that really touches *His* heart? *Romancing the King* is not a book for casual inquirers because once you've read it, then you're responsible for what it says! Brian's book will challenge you out of your old ruts into a deeper relationship with the King—if you're willing! Are you desperate to go much deeper into the heart of the King? Then this book is for you!

It is a message Brian lives and clearly models himself; and out of his deep intimacy with God, he gives you keys on how to romance and touch the heart of the King. Embracing these truths will draw you into a fresh, passionate pursuit of the King's presence, His power, and His purpose for your life. After all, what we pursue is our passion in life! He has laid a strong foundation of the Word, which is interwoven with his own personal experiences and revelation that God has given him.

I have had the privilege of knowing and working with Brian Lake, and I love and respect his walk with God. He is a man of God with sterling integrity, godly principles, one who pursues God in an undistracted way, and a man who loves and honors his wife and children. Brian is a young revivalist who has a heart to see the Church come into a deeper intimacy with Jesus.

Jill Austin
President and Founder
Master Potter Ministries

*E*VERY SUNDAY MORNING AROUND THE world, worship and praise go up before God. It takes on various forms, creeds, styles, and methods. Nevertheless, worship is reserved for God and God alone. Only He is worthy to receive our praise! We are never to worship saints, preachers, prophets, statues, angels, or any other false gods. If we get off focus, we will miss the most important factor of worship—intimacy with God.

Intimacy is a close, personal relationship through which individuals find a conducive atmosphere to share private or personal information. The characteristics necessary to define this relationship determine its value and stability. *Romancing the King* is a description of God's desire to be in relationship and intimacy with humanity. Through invitation, the King of kings invites us to His chamber to experience His glory and presence—like never before.

But do you know what it is like to be in the presence of the King of kings? When you know the King, you will discover what pleases Him! How do you walk through this process? Whatever you pursue becomes your purpose. Are you pursuing the heart of the King? The King of kings is longing for a relationship with you.

Intimacy with the Lord must be our primary focus, not acquiring more of His wealth. The only way to gain access to the splendor of the Kingdom is through a relationship with the King; but unfortunately, many believers' priorities are focused primarily upon the splendor. *Romancing the King* shows believers how to enter His presence.

As revealed in the Book of Esther, Esther was the object of the king's desire. He sought after her. This is how God pursues us, longing to fellowship with us. Like Esther, we are permitted to enter the King's presence because we have been invited and because the King has sought after us.

Discover the purpose of intimacy, worship, and relationship with the King. How do we recognize His invitation? What type of friendship and fellowship is cultivated when we are in the presence of the King? Love, glory, and honor express the nature and character of God, and by spending time with Him, we discover our purpose.

It's time—time for *Romancing the King!*

1

Touching the Heart of the King

The Call to Intimacy

*E*ARLIER IN THE YEAR, I had an experience with the Lord that impacted my life. I saw a simple, yet profound, vision of God's hand extending out and beginning to release great abundance to His people: an abundance of natural wealth and spiritual wealth. God's desire is for all of His children to have *"all sufficiency,"* which includes being made wealthy in everything—our spirits, minds, families, and finances (see 2 Cor. 9:8-11).

God began to reveal that He wanted something deeper and more lasting to form within His people than merely the release of His great abundance. It appeared to me that this release was a mere by-product of some crucial, core value in His people. I saw that, after His great abundance was released, God's hand clearly motioned for His people to come to Him! And, as He beckoned, some came; others did not.

This beckoning represented a call to intimacy—an invitation to access His presence through relationship. Those who chose not to come chose the splendor of the things of the kingdom, but not the King Himself. They were content with the great abundance God had poured out, but they loved the gift more than the giver! The purity and motives of a person's heart were tested through this kingly call.

I remember asking God, "What do You want from me? Do You want me to preach the gospel? Where do You want me to go? What do You really want from me?"

"Brian, I just want your heart," He said.

"So, Lord, You don't really want me to preach the gospel?" I asked.

"No, Brian, that's not what I mean," He answered. "I need you to preach. I need you to tell My people that I just want their hearts. Ask them to seek My face, not My hands."

As He spoke, I was reminded of Psalm 27:8: "'... Seek my face,' my heart said to You, 'Your face, Lord, I will seek'" (NKJV).

Then I heard the Lord say, "In services, many will shed a tear, and that's Me touching their hearts. But how many times have they purposed to touch My heart?"

The Responsibility in Relationship

Friend, many believers have accepted Jesus into their hearts as Lord and Savior, allowing them to have a relationship with Him that contains great potential to touch His heart. Are we willing to accept our responsibility to cultivate this relationship?

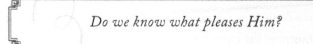

Do we know what pleases Him?

To cultivate a deep and loving relationship with my wife requires that I spend time with her—talking and listening, meeting her needs, and discovering what she likes. Do we do these things with the King of kings? Do we spend time with Him, seeking His face (intimate relationship), or do we just seek His hand (what He can do for us)? Do we know what pleases Him?

When I began to ponder the fact that we need to find out what God likes, He reminded me of the Book of Esther. As I read the biblical account of Esther's life, it was apparent that she stood out from the other young women trying to become queen. Before each young virgin was presented to the king, she was allowed to enter the king's treasury chamber and choose an adornment that she thought would enhance her beauty in his eyes (see Esther 2:13). Each young woman was permitted to carefully examine the splendor of the kingdom: jewels, clothing, gold and silver ornaments, and choose what she thought would please the king.

However, Esther's approach was different.

> *When it was Esther's turn to go to the king, she accepted the advice of Hegai, the eunuch in charge of the harem. She asked for nothing except what he suggested and she was admired by everyone who saw her* (Esther 2:15 NLT).

Rather than choosing among the vast array of displayed riches, Esther wisely chose to seek only that which the king's eunuch, Hegai, advised. She realized that his advice would bring the king's favor since Hegai knew what pleased him. Esther submitted herself in humility to seek the eunuch's advice and to learn what pleased the king.

Do we know what the King of kings likes? Perhaps we need to seek advice from our pastor or friends who have a deep and intimate relationship with the Lord. When we know what the King likes—and we please Him—we will be favored by the Lord, just like Esther!

What are you seeking—the King or His splendor? Which attracts you more—the King's desire for an intimate relationship with you, or His riches and the splendor of His kingdom? Whatever you pursue becomes your purpose. Are you pursuing the heart of the King? The King of kings is longing for a relationship with you, and He is looking for people who are like Esther—those who are not just after His great abundance, but are motivated by a desire to please Him and to know Him.

Intimacy with the Lord must be our primary focus, not acquiring more of His wealth. The only way to gain access to the splendor of the Kingdom is through a relationship with the King; but unfortunately, many believers' priorities are focused primarily upon the splendor. They wait for "more anointing" from God to look better. "Lord, I want this." "Lord, what's in it for me?" We cannot imagine how He feels when His children approach Him only to "get" something.

My own experience with my children speaks volumes. Whenever I give something to them, I wait for a reaction of gratitude and their embrace of love. It means the world to me when they give me a little kiss on the cheek and say, "I love you, Daddy." Some say I spoil my children, but God calls it "blessing." When the cup runs over, some say it is a waste, but God calls it "prosperity." God loves to give to His children, but He wants a relationship with us. He does not want to be treated like Santa Claus.

Gaining Access to the King's Heart

The degree of access we have to God's presence is connected to the depth of our relationship with Him. My children always have access to me. I can be working in my office, talking on the phone, or in a meeting with other people, and if my daughter Molly peeks her little nose through the door, I'll stop everything I'm doing to give her my attention. Her access to me is the result of the deep relationship we share.

The measure of access we have to God is linked to the level of intimacy we have with Him. Esther gained access to the king's heart and found favor.

> *And the king loved Esther above all the women, and she obtained grace and favour in his sight more than all the virgins...* (Esther 2:17).

There were numerous young maidens who were presented to the king, but only one captured his heart because of the essence of who she was. Her humble, surrendered heart toward the king was to him like an invitation to intimacy.

I vividly recall (as if it was yesterday) the day that the girl of my dreams walked into my life. Before I met my wife, I enjoyed going out on the weekends with my friends. But after I met Pamela, whenever my friends called, I didn't hesitate to tell them I had other plans. So what made the difference? Pamela found access to my heart, my mind, and my treasure (or wallet, as I like to tease). Everything about Pamela captured my heart!

When we touch the heart of the true King, we see everything in our lives begin to change. Men and women today want a formula for a powerful encounter with God's presence, but they forget that an encounter comes with relationship. There is no formula.

Dying to Our Desires and Plans

Throughout my life, I have found it necessary to rearrange my schedule to spend time with the ones I love. When I value people and desire to be with them, I am willing to stop whatever I am doing and set aside my plans. Intimacy often requires sacrifice; it calls for us to die to our desires and agendas. The joys and blessings of intimacy are always worth the sacrifice. God made us for relationship; it is what satisfies our souls. However, the greatest satisfaction and joy always comes in the presence of our King. The question is: how badly do we want God's presence? What are we willing to do, to sacrifice, for intimacy with our King?

Esther also needed to sacrifice to come into the king's presence so she could have intimacy with him. Leaving her home to become part of King Ahasuerus's harem could not have been easy for the young girl (see Esther 2:8). Hiding her nationality in order to obey her guardian, Mordecai, must have presented a great challenge (see Esther 2:10). Certainly, Esther longed for fellowship with her own people, missing her Jewish home and culture. Yet, Esther chose to die to those longings, changing her lifestyle to be in the king's presence.

Changes

Imagine what Esther's year of preparation was like. On the surface, it sounds wonderful—twelve months of beautifying! Here is what the year involved:

> *Each young woman's turn came to go in to King Ahasuerus, after she had completed twelve months' preparation, according to the regulations for the woman, for thus were the days of their preparation apportioned: six months with oil of myrrh, and six*

months with perfumes and preparations for beautifying women (Esther 2:12 NKJV).

It appears that Esther was on a spa retreat! However, the royal preparations involved would be quite intimidating for a young peasant girl like Esther. One of the beauty treatments involved six months of bathing in myrrh. Myrrh is derived from a thorn bush and was an ingredient used in the making of perfuming ointments. Although bathing in myrrh caused Esther to be immersed in the florid perfumed scent, culturally and spiritually, this ointment had a far greater significance.

At this time, myrrh was also used to prepare bodies for burial after someone's death. Symbolically, by submitting to the myrrh treatments, Esther demonstrated her willingness to die to herself and her familiar lifestyle in order to be with the king.

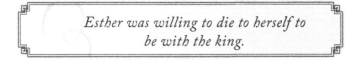

Esther was willing to die to herself to be with the king.

Being of Jewish ancestry, Esther followed her own cultural customs. However, in the king's palace, she was called to act in ways that may have been different and uncomfortable for her—these changes required a change of heart. Esther had to make sacrifices to enable her to go before the king, to gain his favor. She had to exchange her desires for an unfamiliar lifestyle that would prepare her to be desirable to the king, so that he would choose her to reign with him as queen.

Aside from the mandatory twelve-month preparation, what else did Esther do? She sought to learn what the king liked, what he preferred. She inquired of those closest to him on how to please him. She put aside her desires and focused on fulfilling his desires.

In the same way, for believers to have an intimate relationship and enter into the presence of our Divine King, we must die to ourselves, make sacrifices, and face challenges. We also need to discover what He desires and be willing to do whatever it takes to prepare ourselves to enter into His presence.

What would you do if God told you to spend twelve months soaking in oils and spices to prepare for one night with the King Himself? Would you prepare as Esther prepared, and seek to please the King by allowing yourself to be transformed? Would you seek to exude a fragrance that was pleasing for Him? With believers, it is true worship from our hearts that releases a beautiful fragrance, which prepares and positions us for our visit with the King. God loves to manifest Himself in an atmosphere filled with the fragrance of true worship.

Humility Invites Intimacy With the King

Looking back on the vision I had, I saw that the people who chose to come into intimacy with God were lavished with a greater overflow of abundance, in both natural and spiritual wealth. On the other hand, those who did not choose to seek the heart of the King found that their abundance dried up.

In the story of Esther, we learn that, unlike all the other young women who did not interest the king, she possessed an inner beauty that touched his heart. The others could only keep what they had chosen from the treasury. Yet, Esther gained not only the riches and splendor of the kingdom, but the wonderful privilege of close relationship with the king. Her attitude of humility, as well as her ability to die to self, opened the door to intimacy with the king.

Esther's story teaches us some powerful spiritual truths. God wants to pour out the riches of His treasury and His Kingdom on the lives of those who cultivate the same heart as Esther had. The King will freely give us access to His presence, His palace, and His inner chambers when we spend time with Him, putting the desires of His heart first. Then, and only then, will we enter into a deep, intimate relationship with Him. As we truly seek the Kingdom of God, all of the blessings of Heaven will be added to our lives (see Matt. 6:33).

God desires the sacrifice of our lives. He wants our total abandonment to be with Him and to please Him. It is there, in the place of abandoned passion for His presence, that we will touch the heart of the King!

Points to Ponder

1. What is a call to intimacy?

_____

_____

_____

_____

2. How can you gain access to the King's heart?

_____

_____

_____

_____

2

ONE AFTERNOON I WAS HOME alone working in my office. As I sat at my computer, my fingers lightly stroked the keyboard, and my small Maltese dog nuzzled his head contentedly against my feet. Suddenly a presence entered the room with an intensity I had never sensed before. Time seemed to stand still. My dog and I simultaneously turned our heads to see what was happening, to see who was there. Physically I saw nothing. But spiritually, in my mind, I sensed the Spirit of the Lord. I was very aware of my surroundings, yet I could feel God as well.

It was as if I was sleeping, but I was awake, when suddenly I could see in my spirit. I had a vision. I saw Jesus, my Lord and Savior, enveloped in a brilliant white robe. He was not literally in my room, but it felt like it. I saw Him in my mind, yet felt His presence ever so near. That encounter changed my life and forever influenced my life!

In my vision, I could see Jesus standing before me. He did not need to speak. I understood without any verbal communication. It was as if He brought everything I needed, telling me that He had come personally to liberate me. This was the beginning of several visions to follow that brought further revelation to the secrets of "the rooms of the heart."

Later that week, I had a second open vision. In that vision, Jesus led me into a series of rooms, which I later understood to be "rooms of the heart." We walked down a hallway inside an old building lined with doors on each side. The walls were two-toned: dark brown and green. The building was deteriorating, old and smelly. As He led me down the hall, Jesus began to open doors, showing me inside the rooms. Each room was filled with something different. One room was filled with a party atmosphere with sin abounding. Another was packed with sports enthusiasts. Yet another was filled with television sets. And there was a room filled with trophies and "idols." In it, I saw a person polishing his trophies. He turned to see who had opened the door, noticing Jesus, nodded and grinned, then turned away, and continued to polish the trophies.

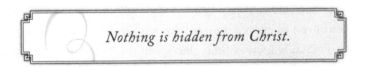

Nothing is hidden from Christ.

I particularly noticed that in all the rooms, some people took a quick glance at Jesus, but immediately returned to what they were doing. It reminded me of the Scripture verse in Ezekiel 8:12 (NKJV) where it says, *"Then He said to me, 'Son of man, have you seen what the elders of the house of Israel do in the dark, every man in the room of his idols?'"* Nothing is hidden from Christ. What happens behind closed doors is always exposed by God's light.

A room is just that, a room. But God looks at our hearts and examines them to discern our intentions and levels of commitment. The Bible says:

> *For the word of God is quick, and powerful, and sharper than any two-edged sword, piercing even to the dividing asunder of soul and spirit, and of the joints and marrow, and is a discerner of the thoughts and intents of the heart* (Hebrews 4:12).

God is saying that it is time for us to purify the rooms in our hearts!

> *Then I commanded them to cleanse the rooms…*(Nehemiah 13:9 NKJV).

Continuing with the vision, every room that Jesus showed me was filled with various things. Jesus said to me, "People ask me to come live in their hearts, but there's nowhere for me to stay."

Jesus then led me to a lower level. This hallway had the appearance of a jail cell—dark, dank, and gloomy with tangled cobwebs and concrete walls. It was a very depressing place. Then He showed me that people had locked themselves in—and locked God out—by listening to the lies of the devil. The devil was the prison guard, feeding the people (mostly women) lies.

Some of the words I heard him say to these people were, "You'll never get out because you're unworthy. What will people think of you? You can never forgive that person. You need to stay in because of the family secret. You're ugly. Hide in here and nobody can hurt you. Remember the abuse? You were raped!"

All of these people seemed very sad and deeply depressed. Sometime later, I had another visitation. The Lord took me into a room likened to a heart filled with the fullness of God. This place was so bright and active! The walls appeared transparent from the sheer brilliance of the light.

As Jesus led me down the hallway, I saw and tangibly felt rooms filled with revelation, love, power, and peace.

And by knowledge shall the chambers [rooms] *be filled with all precious and pleasant riches* (Proverbs 24:4).

I asked the Lord why everything was so transparent looking. He said, "In Me, there is no darkness. In the natural on earth, behind the paint and sheet rock of the walls in your house, there is about four inches of darkness. My light creates transparency and expels all darkness and sin."

Transparent means to allow light to pass through with little or no interruption or distortion, so that objects on the other side can be clearly seen. It is like having the property of transmitting light without appreciable scattering, so that bodies lying beyond are clearly seen.

Psalm 119:130 states, *"The entrance of Your words gives light; it gives understanding to the simple"* (NKJV).

Then the Lord said, "As children of Mine, you must remain transparent."

I then asked the Lord, "Why is it so busy and active here?"

"The richness of My presence is constantly working, producing, creating, and putting into place your destiny and the future of your heart," He replied.

Next Jesus led me into a room that had a window. As we walked toward the window, what I saw next was breathtaking! I beheld the most glorious beauty and sumptuous colors I have ever seen. I could hear a horn like a shofar (a Jewish trumpet) echoing across the beautiful vastness. As I peered through the window, I saw in the distance what appeared to be a beautiful, somewhat elevated, large city ablaze with all the colors in the rainbow intermingled with it. I was viewing the Kingdom: the Kingdom of God is within, and the Kingdom of God is near, within our reach.

> *The time is fulfilled, and the kingdom of God is at hand. Repent, and believe in the gospel* (Mark 1:15 NKJV).

Repent, for the Kingdom of God is at hand!

The Lord said, "I want to show you more." He took me to a huge, rushing waterfall. The source of the waterfall appeared to be a sea that fed it. Then He allowed me to see the waterfall and sea from an aerial view. The waterfall was surrounded by more waterfalls flowing from every side: from the north, south, east, and west. The source of the sea was coming up from beneath the depths of God, the wellsprings, the true Generator of Power. The Lord said, "These are the rivers of living waters springing up from the depths of God Himself, Brian. Praying in the Spirit makes those fountains feeding the sea bubble up even more— releasing a flow out of rivers of revelation, strength, and power."

God is pouring out His Spirit upon the face of the earth.

> *And it shall come to pass in the last days, says God, that I will pour out of my Spirit on all flesh...*(Acts 2:17 NKJV).

The Secret Place

Today, there are increasing miracles, healings, signs, and wonders. God is on the move; He is using available people, for the times we are living in are days of rapid acceleration. God is equipping and releasing His "called" people, restoring finances and relationships. What took years to accomplish in the past is now taking less time.

Even in my ministry, I have seen supernatural growth in a short period of time. One particular individual in ministry said to me, "You have done more in 5 years than what it took me 20 years to do." This person was very anointed and had an intimate relationship with God, but didn't experience the rapid growth I'm now seeing. I believe it is the times we are living in. I believe if that individual would have started his ministry the same time I started mine, he too may have seen more rapid results. Please understand, if you are to see this acceleration, we must maintain a close, intimate union with the King.

Yet, we cannot ignore that evil is intensifying. Darkness seems to increase in intensity as sin runs rampant and lives are destroyed. I sense that God is calling us into a deeper, more intimate friendship and fellowship with Him.

Now, more than ever, it is crucial that we spend more time with God. Without time spent in our "secret place," we are opening up ourselves to more attacks from the enemy. David said:

> One thing have I desired of the Lord, that will I seek after; that I may dwell in the house of the Lord all the days of my life, to behold the beauty of the Lord, and to enquire in His temple (Psalm 27:4).

In order for us to have clean and pure rooms of the heart, we must earnestly seek after Him.

The secret place offers a place of protection from the darkness of the enemy.

> *He who dwells in the **secret place** of the most High shall abide under the shadow of the Almighty* (Psalm 91:1 NKJV).

As we become preoccupied with the busyness of life—sports, work, and entertainment—satan uses these things to distract us from time with God.

Look at this passage in Mark:

> *Give attention to this! Behold, a sower went out to sow. And as he was sowing, some seed fell along the path, and the birds came and ate it up. Other seed [of the same kind] fell on ground full of rocks, where it had not much soil; and at once it sprang up, because it had no depth of soil; And when the sun came up, it was scorched, and because it had not taken root, it withered away. Other seed [of the same kind] fell among thorn plants, and the thistles grew and pressed together and utterly choked and suffocated it, and it yielded no grain. And other seed [of the same kind] fell into good (well-adapted) soil and brought forth grain, growing up and increasing and yielded up to thirty times to thirty times as much, and sixty times as much, and even a hundred times as much had been sown* (Mark 4:3-8 AMP).

In Mark 4:18-19, we find Jesus describing distractions of life in a parable.

> *And the ones sown among the thorns are others who hear the Word; then the cares and anxieties of the world and distractions of the age, and the pleasure and delight and false glamour and*

deceitfulness of riches, and the craving and passionate desire for other things creep in and choke and suffocate the Word, and it becomes fruitless (AMP).

Many Christians are living with cluttered hearts, crowded with things other than God, which makes it difficult to produce the Kingdom of God in our lives or on the earth. Cluttered hearts cannot produce the fruit of healing, miracles, prosperity, joy, peace, or love. How can we help others if we are not producing fruit in our own lives?

The person who maintains the rooms of his heart allows the Holy Spirit to control the pattern of his mind and will produce fruit.

Distractions

The first thing Jesus cited in His description in Mark 4:19 was the cares and anxieties of this world. Webster's Dictionart says: *Cares* are a disquieted state of mixed uncertainty, suffering of mind; grief. *Anxieties* are described as fearful concern, an abnormal and overwhelming sense of fear.

So many people are living in fear and uncertainty. God's Word says:

There is no fear in love; but perfect love casts out fear, because fear involves torment. But he who fears has not been made perfect in love (1 John 4:18 NKJV).

If we have fear in any area of our lives, there must be a deficiency of God's love in that area. Love expels fear. Spending time in His presence develops the love-and-trust relationship that casts out that specific fear.

The second thing Jesus cited in Mark 4:19 was the distractions of this age. The distractions of this age are cunning and subtle tools used by the devil to lure us away from spending time with God. These tools are used by the devil to slowly erode and dismantle your life. John 10:10 declares, *"The thief does not come except to steal, and to kill, and to destroy"* (NKJV). Satan has come to kill, steal, and destroy your life.

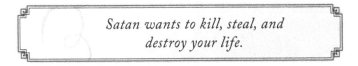

Satan wants to kill, steal, and destroy your life.

Many of us have come to a place where we are treating our Temples like a garbage dump, feeding our spirits trash. Feeding our spirits garbage develops a seed that will produce a multiplied return of rubbish in our lives. How much trash, R-rated television programs, or X-rated movies are in Heaven?

People living distracted lives may say, "Oh, everything is going well," but realize that it is merely a temporary illusion. Failure, disappointment, and destruction are but a thin layer away. Numerous things can become serious pollutants to our minds and bodies: corrupt television, pornography, constant family strife, profane and disrespectful language, speaking words of death, or an imbalance of worldly preoccupations.

God will not compete with your television set or your entertainment. It is not that God has a problem with television; He has a problem that you are choosing it as a priority in your life—over Him. If you are going to walk with God, you must leave behind that which gives you temporary satisfaction.

In Mark 4:19 Jesus also talked about the deceitfulness of riches. His words resound in simplicity and clarity. It all boils down to your priorities. Matthew 6:33 says, *"But seek ye first the kingdom of God, and His righteousness; and all these things shall be added unto you."* Put God first! It is that simple.

The last thing Jesus warns us about is the craving and passionate desire for other things. I feel it is important to say it again. In Psalm 27:4 it says:

> *One thing have I desired of the Lord, that will I seek after; that I may dwell in the house of the Lord all the days of my life, to behold the beauty of the Lord, and to enquire in His temple.*

What is our true desire and our true passion? Are we seeking after God? Are we seeking to have a right heart? It is OK to ask God to restore our passion, to give us a right heart.

> *The spirit of a man is the lamp of the LORD, Searching all the inner depths of his heart.* (Proverbs 20:27 NKJV).

> *He who loves purity of heart and has grace on his lips, the king will be his friend* (Proverbs 22:11 NKJV).

In order to access the window to the Kingdom, we must clean the rooms in our hearts. Then, and only then, will we access the rivers of living waters, revelation, power, and love of the Kingdom.

Points to Ponder

1. What are the rooms in the heart of Jesus?

_____

_____

_____

_____

2. How can you prepare your room to welcome the King?

_____

_____

_____

_____

3

A King's Promise

Created for Fellowship

*I*N THE GARDEN OF EDEN, the Bible says God came to fellowship with Adam and Eve in the "cool of the day" (Gen. 3:8). This phrase is the Hebrew word *reuch*, which is translated "wind, breath, or Spirit" in the Old Testament, and describes the nature of God when He moves. Like the air we breathe, we cannot inhale if God does not exhale. When God manifests, He comes like a "Divine Wind," announcing His arrival so we know when He draws near.

> *In the beginning God created the heaven and the earth. And the earth was without form, and void; and darkness was upon the face of the deep. And the Spirit of God moved upon the face of the waters* (Genesis 1:1-2).

Genesis 1:2 reveals how God moved or hovered over the earth. Before man was created, God hovered. He was waiting for us! The "Glory Cloud" was there, but man was not. The purpose of this cloud was to demonstrate His presence. The purpose of His presence was fellowship—fellowship with humanity.

Our understanding of the nature and function of the Spirit in Genesis 1:2 is informed by Moses' comments in another passage:

He found him in a desert land, and in the waste howling wilderness; He led him about, He instructed him, He kept him as the apple of His eye. As an eagle stirreth up her nest, fluttereth over her young, spreadeth abroad her wings, taketh them, beareth them on her wings (Deuteronomy 32:10-11).

There we are told that God's presence with Israel in the wilderness, the Glory Cloud, is the same Spirit who hovered over the infant creation. The action of the Glory Cloud is that of fluttering, the same word as in Genesis 1:2, and the only other time Moses uses the word. The wilderness is called a "waste," the same word translated "without form" in Genesis 1:2, and again, the only other time Moses uses the word.

The description of the Glory Cloud as fluttering or hovering over Israel with outspread wings is appropriate, not only because of the protective function the Spirit had, but because of the composition of this Divine Cloud. When the prophet Ezekiel penetrates the thick cloud in his vision, the cloud is seen to be alive with winged seraphim and cherubim. The sound of the coming of the cloud is the sound of wings (see Ezek. 1:24; 10:5).

Theologians call this cloud a *"theophany,"* meaning a visible manifestation of God—in this case, the enthroned presence of God with His people. The Old Testament often uses the term *Spirit* as a synonym for *the Cloud,* ascribing the same functions to both (see Neh. 9:19-20; Isa. 4:4-5; Joel 2:28-31; Hag. 2:5).[1]

God's Desire

God has always desired to be close to His creation, especially His greatest delight, humankind. Fellowship with us is God's deepest passion; and for us to fellowship with Him, He must manifest Himself.

Since the fall of Adam and Eve, God has been in passionate pursuit of humanity, revealing Himself in various forms and fashions. He pursued the patriarchs: Abraham, Isaac, Jacob, and Moses, revealing His glory and desiring fellowship. When I say manifest, I mean His presence. It is God's desire to manifest His presence to and through us, as He seeks to draw close—fellowship with His people; dwelling among us.

Man's rebellion continually worked against God's direction. His rebellion was destructive of God's command to perfect the Garden and subdue the whole earth.

It is God's desire to manifest His presence to and through you.

After the sin of man occasioned the destruction of the world at the time of Noah, the Spirit was again there to pass over the earth and separate the land from the water and bring

His people to a Sabbath rest, where the Garden mandate is again given (see Gen. 1:26-28; 8:1,4,15;9:7). A rainbow is set in the Cloud, which is always visible to God (see Ezek. 1:28; Rev. 4:3).

At the time of the Exodus, the Spirit again worked toward re-creation. We have already seen how the Glory Cloud hovered over the people of God, giving them tokens of the new Garden creation, even while in the wilderness. But the most dramatic token of the new Creation was the Tabernacle, under the mountain where the Glory Cloud spoke with Moses.

God's Spirit was His presence with His people, and was both truly present and symbolized by the Tabernacle and the Temple. When you read the portions of Scripture that describe the construction of the Tabernacle and Temple, you begin to see that the Tabernacle, which was itself a picture of an Edenic land, was also filled with the presence of God in the Glory Cloud (see Exod. 40:34-38; 2 Chron. 5:13-14). Throughout the history of redemption, God is present with His people, re-creating the conditions of the Garden.

God revealed His presence to His people in the Cloud of Glory. The cloud functioned as a temporary, chariot-like throne room by which He made His presence known to His people. The Cloud was filled with innumerable angels (see Deut. 33:2; Ps. 68:17), and thus was a revelation of the invisible Heaven where God is seated on His throne of glory, surrounded by His heavenly court and council (see Exod.

24:9-15; Isa. 6:1-4), and from which He spoke to Moses (see Exod. 33:9; Ps. 99:7).

When the Tabernacle was completed, the Spirit Cloud entered it and filled it with the Glory of God (see Exod. 40:34-38; cf. 2 Chron. 5:13-14). Moses, misunderstood by many in our day, was surely understood by his Hebrew readers to be saying that God's saving of His people through the Exodus was a re-creation of the Garden.

God's re-creation of His people in order to bring them into fellowship with Him in the holy mountain of the Promised Land was witnessed by the same manifestation of His creative presence as at the original creation, when the Spirit gloriously arched His canopy over the land.[2]

John tells us that God sent Jesus to manifest the Father in order for God to dwell in us.

And the Word was made flesh, and dwelt among us, (and we beheld His glory, the glory as of the only begotten of the Father,) full of grace and truth (John 1:14).

As a disciple, John beheld Him in the flesh. We, as believers, through the Holy Spirit, can likewise behold His glory, as He reveals Himself through His manifested presence, bringing forth transformation in our lives.

When God Manifests

It is difficult for some believers to conceive why God would manifest Himself. Too often we have looked at ourselves as unholy, unworthy, and insignificant. It is true—in our "unregenerated" state—that we are not worthy to either have a relationship with God or be permitted to dwell in His presence. However, it is God's desire that we commune with Him—not ours.

When the omnipotent, omniscient, omnipresent, eternal, infinite, holy, just, and loving God condescends to manifest Himself, and to touch weak and finite humans, what would we expect or predict might happen to the natural and normal order of things?

There are numerous biblical examples of the manifested presence of God and the responses of those to whom He revealed Himself:

- John 18:6 — Unbelieving guards thrown to the ground.

- Acts 9:4 — Saul of Tarsus saw brilliant light; was thrown from his horse; heard Jesus' voice (audibly), and was temporarily struck blind.

- Revelation 1:17 — John fell as dead, had no bodily strength, and saw and heard into the spirit world.

- Daniel 8:17-19 — Daniel fell; had no strength; terrified by God's Presence.

- 1 Kings 8:10-11 — The priest was unable to stand because of God's glory.

- 2 Chronicles 7:1-3 — Solomon and the priests were unable to stand because of God's glory.

- Acts 10:10; 2 Corinthians 12:1-2 — Peter and Paul fell into trances, seeing and hearing into the spirit world.

- 1 Samuel 19:18-24 — King Saul and his (antagonistic) men are overcome by the Holy Spirit and prophesy as they near the camp of the prophets.

- Exodus 19:16 — Thunder, smoke, shaking of the ground, sounds of trumpets, and voices upon Mount Sinai

- Exodus 34:30 — Moses' face supernaturally shines.

- Matthew 17:2-8 — Jesus and His garment supernaturally shine brilliantly; visitation by Moses and Elijah enveloped in a supernatural cloud.

- Exodus 3:2 — A bush is burning, yet not consumed.

- John 1:32 — The Holy Spirit descends in bodily form as a dove.

- Leviticus 9:24; 1 Kings 18:38; 1 Chron. 21:26 – Holy fire from Heaven consumes sacrifices.

- 2 Corinthians 5:12-13 — Paul describes "beside ourselves" as opposed to being "sober."

- Luke 1:35 — A virgin conceives the Son of God.

Why Manifest?

Why would God manifest Himself to us? How and what does He manifest? Are there any preconditions to His manifestations? Once again, John sheds light on this when he recorded the words of Jesus:

> He who **has My** commandments and **keeps** them, it is he who loves **Me**. And he who loves **Me** will be loved by My Father and I will love him and **manifest** Myself to him (John 14:21 NKJV).

Before we go any further, we must first understand what is meant by the word *manifest*. Manifest means to show or demonstrate plainly; reveal; to be clearly apparent to the sight or understanding; obvious.[3] To manifest is to bring things from the unseen to the seen, from the unheard to the heard, or from the unknown to the known—to reveal something hidden.

Paul said, *"But all things that are reproved are made manifest by the light: for whatsoever doth make manifest is light"* (Eph. 5:13).

When God reveals Himself, He brings something with Him: life and revelation. When He descends upon a location, it flourishes. And, like the Garden of Eden, we will flourish in His atmosphere. The Lord reveals Himself through our minds and senses, replenishing our spirit, giving strength and power.

Nevertheless, why does God choose to manifest? The demonstration and manifestation of God's power points to the God who is beyond us. God wants our faith to rest upon His manifested presence and not the wisdom of men's words (see 1 Cor. 2:4-5).

His manifested presence provides a variety of expression, which demonstrate God's character and brings us into a deeper relationship and levels of maturity:

- Experiential intimacy with God—knowing God and being known by Him.

- Grace and power to overcome inner bondages— fear, lust, pride, envy, greed, deceit, bitterness, etc.

- Impartations of love, peace, joy, fear of God, etc.

- Healings—physical and emotional.

- Bonding experiences with other believers —relational barriers fall when people experience the Spirit's presence together.

- Empowering for ministering to others—anointing for service.

- Release of God's word—prophetic sensitizing, powerful preaching.

- Intercession—apprehended for effective, Spirit-led prayer.

- Enlarging and liberating of spiritual capacities.

The manifestations are given for refreshment, encouragement, and healing. This should lead to deeper discipleship (growth in faith, hope, and love). This should then lead to effective evangelism and, hopefully, full revival.

He loves us deeply and passionately. However, this intense love relationship must be reciprocated to abide. The Bible says, *"If anyone loves Me, he will keep My word; and My Father will love him and We will come unto him and **make Our abode** with him"* (John 14:23).

An abode is a dwelling place, a home or a place to remain in, an invitation for God to come and dwell in our vessel.

Love Is the Key

Every believer wants the presence of God in his or her life. Imagine having God's presence continuously "tabernacling" with us! However, many in the Church are not experiencing this reality. There is a reason; and Jesus did not keep it a secret.

He made it clear that it has to do with our love for Him. Some may declare, "I love Jesus, so why don't I experience His manifested presence?" God's condition for an ongoing experiential reality of His manifest presence is that we are abiding in a *true* love relationship with Him.

The word *love* is used in broad terms in our modern-day society; oftentimes abused. We love to go shopping; we love people; we love sports, food, clothes, entertainers, and the list continues. These are all valid uses of the word in current times. However, it is crucial to understand what kind of love Jesus was talking about.

The apostle John identifies it this way:

> *For this is the love of God, that we keep His command-ments…* (1 John 5:3).
> *This is love that we walk according to His command-ments…* (2 John 6 NKJV).

His promise to manifest Himself is to those who love Him, and those who love Him are not just those who merely *have* His command-ments—they *keep* them as well. All believers have His commandments available by possessing a Bible, but not everyone diligently seeks to learn or keep them.

> *True love is keeping His commandments.*

We can say we love Jesus, singing songs of praise and worship. However, the real evidence of love is not what we say or sing, but rather what we do.

A legalistic view of His words would say we prove our love for Jesus by keeping His commandments. To keep His commandments without a love relationship and a pure heart, conveys the spirit of a Pharisee. This reduces our relationship down to merely works. Wrong thinking!

Jesus simply said the evidence of a person loving Him is that we keep His Word. But it is equally important that we demonstrate our commitment with a heart of obedience and not with an attitude of obligation or a sense of duty.

Lawlessness

If we choose to submit to His will, then we will keep the continuous flow of God's love, resulting in His manifesting presence. However, if we choose *not* to submit to His laws and His will, we will fall short, taking the course of lawlessness.

Lawlessness means to be unrestrained by law; disobedient; unbridled, heedless or contrary to the law.[4]

Furthermore, it is refusing to submit to the law (teachings), God's commandments, and His authority. Jesus foretold what would happen in the days we are living in:

*And because **lawlessness will abound**, the **love** of many **will grow cold**. But he who endures to the end shall be saved* (Matthew 24:12-13 NKJV).

Jesus said lawlessness will abound in the Church in the last days, causing the love of many to grow cold, resulting in a diminished presence of God in their lives and the Church.

Jesus specifically stated *only* those who submit to His commandments or love will experience His manifest presence.

Many souls in the Church have become satisfied without the manifest presence of God. They are in the "comfort zone"—neither too hot, nor too cold. Let us take a closer look at Jesus' words *grow cold* and discover some truths for living.

Consider a cup of tea. It starts out boiling hot; however, if the heat source is removed, over time it grows cooler. It does not become icy cold; rather it becomes "tepid" or "lukewarm," blending in with the same temperature as its surroundings—room temperature. An analogy can be made with today's modern-day church: Many in the church desire to blend in with the world, or fit in with their surroundings—whether it is a "sinful" environment or "church."

Revelation 3:15 says, *"I know your works, that you are neither cold nor hot. I could **wish you were cold or hot**"* (NKJV). Notice that He says works, not good intentions.

There are three types of believers: cold, hot, and lukewarm. What will it take for us to be hot? How can we identify if we are a cold or a lukewarm Christian? Let's find out.

Cold People

The actions of those who are cold toward God are in direct disobedience to His Laws and Commandments. They do not pretend to be something they are not; they are lost in their sin, and they know it. Because Revelation 3:15 is a message addressed to the Church and not the "world," we know the message is for Christians. Therefore, the cold are those who no longer serve Christ in word and deed.

Individuals who grow cold are not serving God, but idols—money, jobs, or pleasure. They have become lovers of the world; people too busy for God, casual church attendees who rarely (if ever) read the Bible or pray.

Hot People

On the contrary, those who are hot are consumed with God, seeking to keep His Word, and walk in obedience and love. They walk in love. They pursue holiness, desiring to be a God-pleaser, not a people-pleaser. You will find them regularly reading the Word, praying, giving to the Lord's work faithfully, and serving in a local church or ministry. They are individuals who are in the process of "dying to self"—fasting and seeking to draw closer to the Lord—and who walk in humility. These individuals are hot because they desire a closer walk with God through a daily walk with the Holy Spirit.

Jesus said, "I wish you were cold or hot." Why would Jesus say this to the Church? He was saying that somewhere in-between was a far worse condition! How could an all-out sinner be in a better position than lukewarm believers? The Bible says, *"So then, because you are lukewarm, neither cold nor hot, I will vomit you out of My mouth"* (Rev. 3:16 NKJV).

Lukewarm

Lukewarm is a blend of hot and cold. A lukewarm person is somewhat like a chameleon transforming into whomever they are associated with. When surrounded by true followers of Jesus, they blend in; but around the world, they mix in. Although they might not serve, they obey God when it is convenient or expedient for their interests and needs.

Why did Jesus use this graphic analogy, to "vomit" a person out if they are lukewarm? In the natural, we vomit what our body cannot assimilate. For instance, if someone ordered a hamburger that was cooked only on the outside, it may look fine to the eye, but if not fully cooked, the person's body would reject the food because it would be harmful to consume and digest. Jesus is actually saying, "I am going to vomit out of My body those who say they belong to Me, but in reality, don't."

Let's be clear—those souls who are either hot or cold are not deceived; they know their condition. However, those who are lukewarm *are* deceived. They believe they are in good standing with God, but their actions betray them. They frequent church, merely going through the motions—singing high praises and shouting "Amen" and return home to become someone else; no prayer and no fellowship. They appear to be hot at church, yet at home and in the world they are cold. That is what is called lukewarm. My friend, this type of attitude has to change!

Get Right or Lose Out

Revelation 3:19 heeds the warning, *"Therefore be zealous and repent"*

(NKJV). The translated Greek word for *repentance* means "to change one's mind."[5] It is a changing of mind about God, about sin, and about one's self. Repenting goes much further than just being sorry for our sin. The *goodness of God* leads us to repentance, and it is produced in us by the Holy Spirit through the Word of God (see Rom. 2:4). The Holy Spirit allows us to feel the weight of our sin before a holy God, thus leading us to turn from sin, change direction, and repent.

Bible repentance is a change of mind prompted by a change of heart, which results in a change of life.

Jesus told a story about a man who had two sons. He said to the first, "Go, work today in my vineyard." The first son said he would not work in his father's vineyard, but Jesus said he later repented and obeyed. What did this boy do when he repented? He simply changed his mind. God wants us to change our minds about sin and our participation in it. This is what the Bible is expressing in commanding all men to repent.

Repentance is a necessary part in becoming a Christian and in living the Christian life. Jesus said in Luke 13:3, *"except ye repent, ye shall all likewise perish."* God wants all who have sinned to repent. He is not willing that any should perish, but that all should come to repentance (see 2 Pet. 3:9).

All Christians have repented of their sins. However, not all who have repented are Christians. Saul of Tarsus is a Bible example of one who believed on Jesus and was "penitent" (see Acts 9:22,26). God sent Ananias to instruct Saul. Ananias said, *"And now why tarriest thou? Arise, and be baptized, and wash away thy sins, calling on the name of the Lord"* (Acts 22:16). Although Saul had repented of his sins, he needed to be baptized into the death of Christ where the cleansing blood was shed; and in this God-ordained way, he needed his sins washed away through calling on the name of the Lord.

The bottom line is we either get right or lose out. If we are not in a right relationship with God, we will not have a visitation or manifestation of His presence. God does not reveal Himself to the prominent, but to the righteous. "Right" living produces precise prophetic moments. We cannot expect God to move into a house that is cluttered, dirty, or preoccupied. We must rearrange the furniture and make room for God to move in! God wants to live in us—not merely rent a room—and reside permanently in our dwelling place. For this to happen, something must transpire.

Before God will show up, we must do something to invite Him. He will not feel at home if we do not make Him welcome. Our "earthen vessel" needs to be fit for a King! The royal presence of God is available. The question: are we ready for Him? Again, what have we done to invite Him? How long will we wait? Now is the time to rearrange our living quarters. Get ready to romance the King.

Next I will reveal the rooms of the heart so we can discover the hidden truths of God. It is time to make residence with our God and King!

Endnotes

1. http://vftonline.org/xmaspiracy/6/presence.htm.

2. Ibid.

3. http://dictionary.reference.com/browse/manifest.

4. http://www.merriam-webster.com/dictionary/lawlessness.

5. W.E. Vine, *Vines Expository Words of Old and New Testament* (Iowa Falls, Iowa: World Bible Publishers), 280.

Points to Ponder

1. How does God manifest His presence?

_____

_____

_____

_____

2. Why does God manifest His presence?

_____

_____

_____

_____

3. What are the keys to experiencing His presence?

_____

_____

_____

4

A Living Fellowship With God

WHAT DOES IT TAKE TO begin a relationship with God? Is it to devote yourself to unselfish religious deeds? Is it to attempt to become a better person, so that God will accept you? Can a person actually embark on a journey that leads to knowing God? The overwhelming claim of the Bible is *yes!* Not only can we know the Lord and the Creator of everything that exists, we are invited—even urged—to know Him intimately, personally, and deeply.

It is certainly evident today that the majority of people in the world neither knows, nor wants to know, the living God. The masses are totally indifferent to the One by whom all life is given. They think that if He exists at all, He is unimportant and irrelevant.

Some claim to know God, or they say they are "seeking him." The quality of their lives, though, shouts that the Lord of glory is a disappointing, uninteresting Person, and His presence cannot be experienced in a practical or personal way. Still others pursue representing God (or rather *misrepresenting* Him), as a way to get rich quick or to gain power and influence in the world. Although avowed atheists seem to be few in numbers, religious confusion abounds; and it is clear that not many enjoy the intimate relationship God created them to experience.

Yet God is the ultimate reality in the entire universe, and as the apostle Paul says, *"For of Him and through Him and to Him are all things, to whom be glory forever"* (Rom. 11:36 NKJV). Those who genuinely desire to know Him (as He really is) are never disappointed. In one sense, knowing God is the easiest thing in the world, easier than falling off a log. Indeed, the Bible says simply, *"Draw near to God and He will draw near to you"* (James 4:8 NKJV), and again, *"Ask and it will be given you, seek and you shall find, knock and it will be opened to you"* (Matt. 7:7 NKJV). Jesus said:

> *Come to Me all you who labor and are heavy laden and I will give you rest. Take My yoke upon you and learn from Me for I am gentle and lowly of heart, and you will find rest for your souls. For yoke is easy and My burden is light* (Matthew 11:28-30 NKJV).

In another sense, knowing and loving God is a lifetime process that follows that initial introduction we call regeneration, or the "new birth." However, there are many pitfalls and difficulties in following God on a long-term basis. Many enthusiastic seekers eventually drop out and fall along the wayside. Others shipwreck their lives, "writing God off," failing to see the depths of His mercy and His ability to save and repair damaged lives.

But it is He who said to Israel, *"All day long I have stretched out my hands to a disobedient and contrary people"* (Rom. 10:21 NKJV). What is needed is a sure word, a clear instruction on how to know God and how to build a solid foundation for a life lived in fellowship and harmony with Him.

> *But also for this very reason, giving all diligence, add to your faith virtue, to virtue knowledge, to knowledge self-control, to self-control perseverance, to perseverance godliness, to godliness brotherly kindness, and to brotherly kindness love* (2 Peter 1:5-7 NKJV).

These attributes begin with faith and end with love. The journey to know God will begin when we develop these virtues. Most people know little about God or the Bible when they become Christians. Somehow, we manage to reach out and place our trust in Jesus, which allows God to respond to us. He never comes into a human heart uninvited.

Obviously, the list of virtues is not something we work through once, and then stop; it is a pattern for day-to-day living for the rest of our lives. Peter is not telling us how to be saved by good works, but rather about giving God the opportunity to mold us into the likeness of His Son.

> *…work out your own salvation with fear and trembling; for it is God who works in you both to will and to do for His good pleasure* (Philippians 2:12-13 NKJV).

Seven Steps

The first step to working out our own salvation is ***faith***. When we act in faith, God responds. The Bible says, *"Without faith it is impossible to please God"* (Heb. 11:6). Every virtue must be founded upon a measure of faith. It is the foundation for every action with God. Faith is the necessary ingredient to activate the spiritual laws through which they receive. Hebrews 11:6 continues, *"For he that cometh to God must believe that He is, and that He is a rewarder of them that diligently seek Him."*

Step two is **virtue**, which means that our newfound relationship with Christ will lead us to make changes in our lifestyle. As mentioned previously, *repentance* means to have a different mind, to see things differently and to change our behavior accordingly. Knowing Jesus changes our priorities. We abandon old habits and change activities. New friends come into our lives and other deleterious relationships end. We start to *"try to learn what is pleasing to the Lord"* (see Col. 1:10).

Step three asks us to acquire further **knowledge**. As we apply the truth we have received, it becomes part of who we are, broadening our capacity to acquire new and deeper truth. However, truth not acted upon is lost. Christians must never stop learning and growing!

> *All Scripture is God-breathed and is useful for teaching, rebuking, correcting and training in righteousness, so that the man of God may be thoroughly equipped for every good work* (2 Timothy 3:16-17 NIV).

When we plateau in the Christian life, believing we now know enough to get by, we may find ourselves running on autopilot, no longer exercising genuine faith. Real faith is always reaching out in trust for that which is beyond our immediate grasp—whatever is not based on faith is sin. Therefore, standing still in the Christian life actually causes us to lose ground. Treading water upstream from the Falls (in the Niagara River) is not recommended!

> *Talk no more so very proudly, let no arrogance come from your mouth; for the Lord is a God of knowledge, and by Him actions are weighed* (1 Samuel 2:3 NKJV).

Self-control, step four, is actually part of the fruit of the Spirit.

But the fruit of the Spirit is love, joy, peace, longsuffering, gentle-ness, goodness, faith, meekness, temperance: against such there is no law. And they that are Christ's have crucified the flesh with the affections and lusts. If we live in the Spirit, let us also walk in the Spirit. Let us not be desirous of vain glory, provoking one another, envying one another (Galatians 5:22-26).

As we mature in Christ, we become reliable, dependable, and con-sistent; patiently enduring.

Step five is to be ***steadfast***. We keep our promises and stop the roller-coaster living that often marks our early Christian life. Jesus said, *"If you abide in My word, you are My disciples indeed. And you shall know the truth, and the truth shall make you free"* (John 8:31-32 NKJV).

Step six is ***godliness***. William Barclay says, "The word is *eusebeia* and is quite untranslatable. Even piety is inadequate, carrying as it does a suggestion sometimes of something not altogether attractive. The great characteristic of eusebeia is that it looks in two directions. The man who has eusebeia always correctly worships God and gives Him His due; but he always correctly serves his fellowmen and gives them their due. The man who is eusebes (the corresponding adjec-tive) is in a right relationship both with God and with his fellowmen. Eusebeia is piety but in its most practical aspect. Eusebeia is the near-est Greek word for religion; when we begin to define it, we see the intensely practical character of the Christian religion. When a man becomes a Christian, he acknowledges a double duty, to God and to his fellow men."[1]

Finally, step seven is ***love***. It is by faith that we discover how to show brotherly concern and affection toward other believers. The self-giving love, which comes from God, is last on the list. Godly love does not depend on our emotions. We love by exercising faith—trusting in God—even as we apprehend the other listed attributes of virtues, by faith.

> With virtue, there is no standing still; anyone who does not advance daily loses ground. To remain at a standstill is impossible; he that gains not, loses; he that ascends not, descends. If one does not ascend the ladder, one must descend; if one does not conquer, one will be conquered.
>
> — Saint Bonaventure (1221-1274)

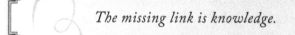

The missing link is knowledge.

These seven steps help guide us into a deeper relationship with God. Fellowship with the Holy Spirit is increased and our commitment is sealed. Paul says it best:

> *For this reason I also suffer these things; nevertheless I am not ashamed, for I know whom I have believed and am persuaded that He is able to keep what I have committed to Him until that day* (2 Timothy 1:12 NKJV).

What Do You Know?

Throughout history, people have dreamt of making life perfect, but no one has been able to do it. Politicians promise a better life for all their constituents if they win office, but their greatest skill seems to be spending vast amounts of money. Scientists often predict a new world will come from their research, and yes, modern technology has improved life in many ways. Yet science has equally brought us brutal weapons of war, high-pressure working conditions, and devastating pollution.

In fact, the world is now in serious trouble, particularly in the area of human relations. Sexual perversions are widely accepted. Many marriages are troubled and brief, and children are neglected and abused. Even young children commit violent crimes with no trace of pity or remorse. Ethnic and religious wars rage on for years. Billions of decent, hardworking people live in miserable poverty, while others (who appear to work with ease) live in luxury. Something is missing. The missing link is knowledge—of God. Without Him we are hopeless and helpless, going through life empty, without purpose and life.

What is life? If life has a purpose, then there must be a "Purposer," One who brought life into existence for a reason. Further, in creating life, this One would have designed it able to fulfill that purpose.

Humanity has always instinctively sensed that there is a higher power or deity. That is why there is no culture on earth lacking a religious tradition. There are thousands of religions worldwide with most involving minor variations of beliefs or ritual. There are perhaps seven major branches of religion, encompassing more significant differences in belief, yet even these teach similar ideas. Can God be found in any or all of them?

Every religion attempts to explain the purpose of life in some way, although a few claim there is no real "purpose" as such. For example, the Hindu religion teaches reincarnation, whereby life is a continual cycle of birth, death, and rebirth, ending, if ever, only in a state of nothingness or unconsciousness. In this view, any one individual cannot hope to live forever as himself, having a lasting purpose as an individual. Other religions say that the purpose of life is to be saved and go to Heaven at death. One teaches that we all may become gods in time if we do well.

> The word "religion" is extremely rare in the New Testament and the writings of mystics. Those attitudes and practices to which we give the collective name of religion are not represented in our modern-day vernacular. To be religious is to have one's attention fixed on God and on one's neighbor, in relation to God. Therefore, almost by definition, a "religious" man is not thinking about religion; he hasn't the time. Religion is what we (or he himself at a later moment) call his activity from outside.
>
> —C.S. Lewis (1898-1963), "Lilies that Fester"

Religion is so complex and confusing that many today choose not to discuss it. They may say, "You believe what you want to believe, I'll believe what I want, and we'll both be happy." This is a tolerant, relaxed philosophy, and is certainly better than fighting. But should we be satisfied with that as the best possible solution? What is the key to eternal life? Knowing God.

Jesus, who is universally known throughout the world as a man who claimed to be sent by God, said He had come to *"bear witness to the truth"* (John 18:37 NKJV). This prompted a skeptical, worldly wise man, Pontius Pilate, to retort, *"What is truth?"* Apparently, he felt like many do today, that no one could claim to know the truth. Was he right?

Where and how should one search for truth about God and the meaning of life? A scientist doing research considers what he knows already to establish a reasonable course of inquiry. We have already looked at creation, which tells us a few valuable things about its Designer. He must have tremendous power. He is very precise; all things work together according to exact laws. He has a sense of beauty and a sense of humor. He must be infinitely more intelligent than we are.

But here we have an advantage over the scientist. God is no mere rock or animal, even though some religions depict Him that way (see Rom. 1:22-23). He can rightly be expected to speak up and make Himself known. Therefore, in our search, we should seek to communicate with Him.

To discover the purpose and meaning of life, we must know God! This is why we were created—to know Him. *"And this is eternal life, that they may know You, the only true God, and Jesus Christ whom You have sent"* (John 17:3 NKJV).

Eternal life reverses the curse of sin. Sickness is a manifestation of spiritual death. (If the body is overcome by sickness, it will die.) Sickness and disease has a force behind it, the power and force of death. Healing is a manifestation of life that comes from God, the manifestation of spiritual life in the physical body.

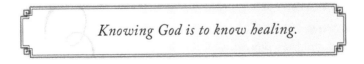

Knowing God is to know healing.

Knowing God is to know healing. When you know Him, you will experience all that He is—His joy, peace, favor, faithfulness, goodness, and His healing. A revelation of healing assures you that *your faith will make you whole.*

It is not up to God's power for you to be healed; He has enough power to heal us all. Your faith will make you whole; according to your faith, the Scriptures stress, as you have believed. Jesus emphasized *your* faith.

Your Faith

What is faith? I believe in the power of confession and the necessity of knowing the Word. However, I am increasingly aware that many people know very little about faith and how it works. We can have lots of tapes, DVDs, and bumper stickers, but that does not mean you live by faith. So what, then, is faith?

Many quote Hebrews 11:1, *"Now faith is the substance of things hoped for, the evidence of things not seen"* (NKJV).

That is only one aspect of faith. The writer of Hebrews continues, verse after verse, telling us what faith is. Verse 1 alone does not fully describe the concept of faith. What Abraham, Enoch, Noah, David, and Samuel all had in common—they *knew* Jehovah. Their faith came from knowing God.

Faith works the same in every area, whether it is in healing or prosperity. Faith has to be *developed* in each area. Simply because you have faith in healing does not mean you have faith that is developed in finances, ministry, prosperity, or for divine direction. What that means is that we have to get to know God as our Provider, Healer, Protector, and Director. When we get to know Him intimately and passionately, then we have discovered the essentials of life. Then our faith will take on a new dynamic. It will begin to change everything about us. The Bible says in Mark 11:22-24:

And Jesus answering saith unto them, Have faith in God.
For verily I say unto you, That whosoever shall say unto this
mountain, Be thou removed, and be thou cast into the sea;
and shall not doubt in his heart, but shall believe that those
things which he saith shall come to pass; he shall have whatso-
ever he saith. Therefore I say unto you, What things soever ye
desire, when ye pray, believe that ye receive them, and ye shall
have them.

You cannot have faith in God beyond the degree of your relationship. Simply stated, if you do not really know Him, you cannot go
deeper in your relationship with Him.

Do you realize that it is possible to know Scriptures and not know
God? We can go to conferences, acquire biblical books and tapes, and
not ever really *know* Him.

And ye have not His word abiding in you: for whom He
hath sent, Him ye believe not. Search the scriptures; for
in them ye think ye have eternal life: and they are they
which testify of Me (John 5:38-39).

The religious leaders had Jesus in the midst of them, and yet
they did not know Him. They were the "word people" of their day.
Despite their ability to memorize the Torah, they did not know the
God of the Word.

This implies that we can search the Scriptures and think we have
eternal life. It is more than that. We can be deceived by thinking that
we are "all right." But do we know what it is to have eternal life? What
is eternal life?

It is not just about going to Heaven, it is knowing God.

How Do You Know You Know?

We need to hear God for ourselves. It is too easy for today's Christian to "eat off someone else's plate." We cannot grow in our relationship with God through preaching only, or through what someone else tells us about God. We may have "head knowledge," but we have not developed "heart knowledge." We need to stop living in someone else's revelation.

> And many of the Samaritans of that city believed on him for the saying of the woman, which testified, He told me all that ever I did. So when the Samaritans were come unto Him, they besought Him that He would tarry with them: and He abode there two days. And many more believed because of His own word; and said unto the woman, Now we believe, not because of thy saying: for we have heard Him ourselves, and know that this is indeed the Christ, the Saviour of the world (John 4:39-42).

Many of the Samaritans of the city believed in Him because of the word of the woman's testimony. Then Jesus showed up. And they said to the woman, "Now we believe, not because of what you said, for we ourselves have heard Him and we know that this is indeed the Christ, the Savior of the world." Instead of just reading the Scriptures, I want to know the One who spoke it.

In a relationship, we get to know the person we are in fellowship with. Fellowship builds trust. It is difficult to trust someone beyond the extent of how well you know him or her. But what is relationship without fellowship? Fellowship is the *joy of relationship*.

God satisfies our spiritual appetite.

The more you have in common, the more fellowship you will have. For example, friends who like to hunt or cook will frequently talk about hunting or cooking because they have those things in common.

So what do Christians have in common? Do we hate sin? Do we walk in love? Do we have a giving heart? Is our life Christ-like?

How we talk will determine how we live. Do we look like Him? These are all indicators of our romance with Him.

A divine romance needs to develop between humankind and God. Romance is the sacred relationship acquired in prayer and worship. But it is not just setting an egg timer and when the bell rings we are done. It is necessary to develop a contemplative prayer life.

A contemplative prayer life is obtained through reflection, full or deep consideration. It is a listening prayer; more listening and less talking. We are attentive with our ears tuned in to the Father. It is a communication all its own. We go before Him just to listen. And when we learn to listen, He satisfies our spiritual appetite.

Jesus said, *"If anyone thirsts, let him come to Me and drink"* (John 7:37 NKJV). In the natural, we drink all the time, not merely once a week. Our body needs nourishment; likewise, so does our spiritual body. The Bible says, *"Taste and see that the Lord is good"* (Ps. 34:8). If we do not get quiet before God in the secret place, we will never discover His goodness.

What Should You Know?

If we do not learn what it takes to know God, we will pass on an apathetic lifestyle to the next generation. Teenagers are facing pressures today, and if we do not guide them, they will follow a path of destruction.

It is best to teach them when they are young, as they may never learn how to romance the King. So what do we need to know to guide our children into fellowship with God and developing intimacy with Him? Being aware of the following four aspects will help:

1. Know the enemy's arsenal, weapons of mass destruction:

   - Entertainment, with no boundaries

   - Cell phones, without limitations

   - Internet, without restrictions

   - Excessive TV, without parental control

   How can today's youth experience the fullness of joy if they are too busy for God or distracted by life's pleasures? Today's society is running a fast course toward hell. We need to slow down. The Bible says, *"Be still, and know that I am God"* (Ps. 46:10). To *be still* means to remain in a place of rest, or to remain free from turbulence or commotion. If the pace is too fast or the volume too loud, how can we hear God speak?

   There is more than one level of stillness. And to be still does not mean you are not moving forward. To be still means we know God is on the throne, and He's not nervous. We are still (not panicking) because we *know God!*

We know God is our Provider, Healer, and our heavenly Father. When Jesus was transfigured on the mountain, the Bible says in Matthew, *"His face shone like the sun, and His clothes became as white as the light"* (Matt. 17:2 NKJV). In all His glory, God spoke and said, *"This is My beloved son, in whom I am well pleased, **Hear** Him"* (Matt. 17:5 NKJV).

Even in all His glory, God thought it so important to tell Jesus who He was—His Son. That is intimacy.

The enemy uses many things to distract young people and adults alike. Today's current culture is an over-stimulated information age, complete with cell phones, e-mail, palm pilots, and laptops. But can they—can you—*hear Him?*

We need to know that simple distractions can prevent people from hearing God speak. Purpose-filled prayer is available to anyone, anywhere, at anytime. We can become a portable sanctuary. Even in class, meetings, or during mealtime, if we are quiet, it gives God the opportunity to break in and say something. But are we so conditioned to our busy lifestyles, so that we cannot hear God when He speaks? God help us.

2. Fear of Silence

Even when we are home alone at night, many people turn on the television or radio because it's "too quiet." Our Western culture has produced a music/sound mentality to soothe our minds. Is your house filled with television sounds in three rooms? Are stereos blasting down the hallway, with the Internet broadcasting the latest You Tube video, or is your home and mind filled with the presence of the King? The extraneous noise keeps your mind from being idle, but it also prevents you from meditating on God or His Word.

Getting quiet is the first step to, *"Be still and know that I am God."* If we cannot get quiet, we cannot become still—and if we do not become still, we will not be able to hear God speak. What are we afraid of? *Really* hearing things? When we get quiet, we have to deal with ourselves. We may have to deal with the voice of God as He begins to reveal things to us that need to be changed and rearranged in our life.

If silence is a condition of this experience with God, many people will fall because it seems to be a major undertaking for most Christians. However, if we do not become still, we will never spend time in the presence of God. If we take the time, we will reap the benefits. Time develops intimacy; intimacy breeds revelation, and revelation will always demand change in our life.

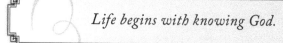

Life begins with knowing God.

3. Learn the Vocabulary of Silence

Habakkuk 2:20 says, *"The Lord is in His holy temple; let*

*all the earth **be silent** before Him"* (NIV). Job 33:31-33 reminds us, *"Listen to me; be silent, and I will speak…listen to me; be silent; and I will teach you wisdom"* (NIV).

Saint Teresa of Avila (1515-1582) was similar to contemporary Christians in her desire to seek God through prayer, but felt her time with Him too brief. Teresa wanted to talk to God four hours a day. For most of us, it is hard to pray even an hour. We pray for everything in five minutes and think we have spent time with God.

I understand her desire. Saint Teresa said, "God, I want You to make me pray four hours a day."

God said to her, "Teresa, I don't make the little birds eat. When birds get hungry, they eat, and when you are hungry for Me, you will spend more time with Me and enjoy it without measuring it or watching the clock."[2]

Why can't we set the time aside for Him? Have we lost our "first love"? Are we not hungry for Him anymore?

Saint Julian of Norwich (1342-ca.1416) claimed to have had a revelation from God when she was in her twenties, which she wrote about. She said God told her to pick up a chestnut. When she did, God said to her, "All the great truths can be found in a chestnut." After 25 years of contemplative prayer, she wrote about it again and had this to say about the chestnut: "God made it, God sustains it, and God loves it."[3]

4. Listening to God

There is a difference between *hearing* and *listening*. We often hear the voices of people around us and birds singing, yet we remain focused on our own situation. Even as we read a book, our mind is not focused on these background sounds. Listening, on the other hand, is when our thoughts are centered on what our ears are hearing; it is tuning in with our heart *and* mind. We cannot fellowship with God if it is not a lifestyle. Living fellowship is necessary, not merely occasional fellowship, to develop intimacy.

Do you want to *know* God? Do you want to learn how to develop a living fellowship with the King? It begins with knowing God.

Endnotes

1. William Barclay, *Letters of James and Peter*, *The New Daily Study Bible* (Louisville, KY: Westminister John Knox Press, 1975, 2003), 350.

2. http://www.doctorsofthecatholicchurch.com/TA.html.

3. http://en.wikipedia.org/wiki/Julian_of_Norwich.

Points to Ponder

1. What are the necessary ingredients to develop a relationship with God?

_____

_____

_____

_____

2. How does faith operate in worship?

_____

_____

_____

_____

5

True Worship Touches His Heart

*I*N THE LAST FIFTEEN TO twenty years, the Church has sounded the trumpet, calling His worshipers to worship Him in Spirit and in truth. David worshiped with instruments and joyful singing, dancing, shouting, and rejoicing before the Lord of hosts. Today, we have liberty in our worship, for where the Spirit of the Lord is, there is liberty! We are excellent in singing, playing instruments, and the dance. These are all great and marvelous things, which the Spirit has revealed to His Church. Our God is enthroned upon the praises of His people!

While these are glorious things, we cannot live in the past. God, our Father, desires that we open our spiritual eyes to see more and more of His marvelous nature. Today, we may ask, what is He revealing to us now?

When His Cloud of Glory moves forward, then we must move with Him.

Beautiful voices blended in harmony, singing praises to God, is heavenly music to our ears. Anointed musicians playing skillfully on their instruments, as a symphony of praise to God, cause us to rejoice. Although these forms of worship are wonderful, they must not become our only focus. Our focus is not to be only on our instruments, songs, or style of worship. *Our focus is to be on the One who sits on the throne!*

What Is Worship?

Worship is not music. Worship is not a song. Worship is our lives presented to our God as living sacrifices each day that we have breath and throughout eternity. God is Spirit, and we must worship Him in Spirit and in truth. We are spirit beings created by God to worship Him. We worship Him in and by His Spirit within us. All that we do is worship unto our God. It is not just a song that pleases God, but our lives devoted and offered wholly unto Him, which brings Him joy.

Many times, we become focused on things and on doing, rather than on being who He created us to be. We make everything, even our worship, so complicated. Let us return to the simplicity of worship. It is not our excellent musicianship that exalts the Lord, but the broken and contrite heart that honors and glorifies Him.

> *Your life devoted and offered wholly to Him brings Him joy.*

Yes, we desire to excel in our musicianship, because He deserves our best. But this is not our focus. As we read and study the worship of

Revelation, we see that the Lamb who sits upon the throne is the center of everything. His Kingdom consumes all other kingdoms. He is our all in all, and is worthy to be praised!

He is the One who purchased men and women from every tribe and nation through His Blood. He is the All-Powerful God, Sovereign Ruler. As we look unto Jesus, the Author and Finisher of our faith, our response is to bow in worship to His majesty.

Let us hear the sounding of His trumpet in this day. He alone is the central focus of our lives and our worship. Though He is moving in miraculous wonders among the people of the earth, and though He blesses His people with good things, we do not worship Him for these things—we worship Him because of *who* He is. Both now and forevermore, we worship His majesty!

> *One thing I have desired of the Lord that I will seek that I may dwell in the house of the Lord all the days of my life, to behold the beauty of the Lord and to inquire in His temple. For in the time of trouble He shall hide me in His pavilion. In the secret place* [the inner chambers of His palace] *of His tabernacle He shall hide me; He shall set me high upon a rock. And now my head shall be lifted up above my enemies all around me: Therefore I will offer sacrifices of joy in His tabernacle; I will offer sacrifices of joy in His tabernacle; I will sing praises to the Lord* (Psalm 27:4-6 NKJV).

As mentioned previously and worth repeating, worship and praise is reserved only for God. Only He is worthy, not any of His servants (see Rev. 19:10). We are never to worship saints, prophets, statues, angels, or any other false gods. And we should never worship merely to expect something from Him in return. We should worship God because He deserves it and for His pleasure alone. Worship can be public praise to God in a congregational setting, where we can proclaim (through music and praise) our adoration and thankfulness for Him and what He has done for us (see Ps. 22:22; 35:18).

True worship is felt inwardly, and then comes out through our actions. "Going through the motions" simply done from a sense of obligation is displeasing to God and in vain. He can see through all the hypocrisy, and He hates it. He demonstrates this in Amos 5:21-24 as He talks about coming judgment.

Another example is the story of Cain and Abel, sons of our first parents, Adam and Eve. Both men brought gift offerings to the Lord, but He was only pleased with Abel's offering. Cain brought the gift out of obligation. Abel brought the finest lambs from his flock, and offered to the Lord gifts from a heart filled with love, faith, and admiration for God (see Gen. 4:4-6).

Your worship glorifies and exalts God.

True worship is not confined to singing in church, or open praise (although these things are both good and we are instructed to do them in the Bible); instead, true worship is the acknowledgment of God and all His power and glory in all we do. To enter into this, we must know God; we cannot be ignorant of Him (see Acts 17:23). Worship glorifies and exalts God and shows our loyalty and admiration to the King.

There are several points to be aware of in order to develop and enter into deep worship with the King:

- Never underestimate the potential of one worship encounter.

- Expect God to show up every time.

- Be patient and wait upon the Lord.

- Focus your mind upon Jesus.

- Open the door of your heart to God.

- Ten seconds in the presence of the King can change your destiny forever (just like Esther; it changed her from a peasant to a princess in one night).

The Fragrance of Worship

Now when every maid's turn was come to go in to king Ahasuerus, after that she had been twelve months, according to the manner of the women, (for so were the days of their purifications accomplished, to wit, six months with oil of myrrh, and six months with sweet odours, and with other things for the purifying of the women) (Esther 2:12).

For twelve months, Esther bathed in oils and perfumes to transform the fragrance of her body. Matthew Henry describes this event:

We see to what absurd practices those came, who were destitute of Divine revelation, and what need there was of the gospel of Christ, to purify men from the lusts of the flesh, and to bring them back to the original institution of marriage. Esther was preferred as queen. Those who suggest that Esther committed sin to come at this dignity do not consider the custom of those times and countries. Everyone that the king took was married to him, and was his wife, though of a lower rank. But how low is human nature sunk, when such as these are the leading pursuits and highest worldly happiness of men! Disappointment and vexation must follow; and he most wisely consults his enjoyment, even in this present life, who most exactly obeys the precepts of the Divine law. But let us turn to consider the wise and merciful providence of God, carrying on his deep but holy designs in the midst of all this. And let no change in our condition be a pretext for forgetting our duties to parents, or the friends who have stood in their place.[1]

Worship covers us with the fragrance of the King. When we are consumed with worship, we can become engulfed in His presence. I have been in services when we could smell the fragrance of God permeating the room. The oils and perfumes Esther used belonged to the Kings. She did not bring her own oils; they were supplied to her.

Worship is to be directed unto the King, and not for our entertainment. The oil and its fragrance are supplied with the presence of the King through the act of intimate worship. It is like the aroma from the incense in the Holy Place, a pleasing smell unto God.

Likewise, we must soak in the King's oils and perfumes to "smell" like the King, which is only accomplished as we are in His divine presence. We cannot expect His presence to come through entertainment or "canned" worship, regardless of how perfected the sound. To be a skilled musician does not depend on the number of years the person has successfully played an instrument. If that was the case, we could bring secular bands from nightclubs into our churches to lead worship. It is more than a song—it is the attitude, heart, and spirit upon which it is delivered.

In order to attract the King, we must worship in a way that generates an atmosphere that is inviting to God. Too often, worship leaders or churches select their style of songs according to the church attendees. Song selection is too often determined by satisfying significant, prominent, or influential members who may object to a different sound. But who are we worshiping? People or God? God is our audience! Our goal and desire should be to invite the King into our time of worship.

I chose a certain brand of cologne to wear because the aroma is pleasant. But my decision to purchase it was not based upon my preference, but rather upon the direction of my wife, Pam, and what she found pleasing. The same analogy applies to worshiping God. We are to attract Him. That is the difference between a worship encounter versus a church songfest. Our goal should be to smell like the King. In order to enter a heavenly atmosphere of the King's palace, we must *smell* heavenly, not earthly.

Consider when you are expecting houseguests. Before they arrive, you may light candles or turn on the potpourri pot to enhance the atmosphere with a welcoming fragrance. How many times have you driven by a farm with animals such as cows or pigs, and practically gagged from the smell? Farmers often have separate changing quarters to change from their work clothes before they enter their house because of this foul odor.

I have a business that involves the hog industry. I guarantee that many in church would object if I entered the building smelling like a pig! As pungent as the odor of pigs and cows may be, farmers adjust to the smell. I wonder if that may be happening in our churches today. Have we adjusted to the noxious smell (of our form of worship) and assumed it is good, when in actuality it is a stench in the nostrils of the Lord?

You are permitted to enter His presence.

Jesus, the King, desires not only to attend our church services and private times of worship, but He longs to dwell in our midst. And at times, He may visit. But if the atmosphere is not conducive, He will not remain. God loves to manifest His presence and reveal His secrets in an atmosphere filled with the fragrance of worship. He comes to our meetings only in response to our worship and hunger, attracted to our desperation and holy hunger for His visitation. But are we willing to do what it takes? The Bible says:

> But the hour cometh, and now is, when the true worshippers shall worship the Father in spirit and in truth: for the Father seeketh such to worship Him. God is a Spirit: and they that worship Him must worship Him in spirit and in truth (John 4:23-24).

The Father is not seeking apostles or prophets, pastors, teachers, or evangelists. He is seeking worshipers worshiping in Spirit and in truth.

God spoke this to me once, "Brian, when you enter true worship, that is where I [God] will give you whatever you desire. And many will make their request known to Me and many have. But only a rare few will ask what I want."

Our desires will be met when we enter into His presence. Esther, as revealed in the Book of Esther, was the object of the king's desire. He sought after her. This is how God pursues us, longing to fellowship with us. We are permitted to enter His presence because we have been invited, and because the King has sought after us.

How many times have we gone to the King of kings simply because we needed something? We must grieve the Lord when we only come to Him to *get*. How many times have we gone to Him just to fellowship? We must purpose to touch His heart. Is our intention to leave church services feeling "blessed," or is it to bless the Lord?

What would worship in the house of God be like if we viewed it like a "date" with God? Perhaps we would prepare and act differently. In every service, the Holy Spirit has set a level for us to ascend to; a higher level in worship. Once there, a fragrance covers the throne, and the Holy Spirit begins to touch, heal, and change people's lives, because He is "filling" or inhabiting the room.

I remember one of my more profound services. I was ministering in a small, packed-full church in Guatemala. The worship was different. You could feel it penetrating your heart. The quality of the worship was only average, but the whole place was so focused on worshiping Jesus, everyone seemed to come into one accord. A heavy, holy presence filled the place with a reverent atmosphere. The people began to weep, falling on their faces, the altar was full with people repenting and worshiping God. Many of the people testified that they could smell a fragrance—the fragrance of the King. Many received healings and miracles just by being in the atmosphere. Later, I heard a report of a couple that owned a business, which was robbed days before the meeting. Their business was failing. After they attended the meeting, God restored their business and it began to prosper abundantly. The atmosphere alone changed their lives and their business.

This was the case with the woman who came to anoint the Master's feet. The Bible says:

There came a woman having an alabaster box of ointment of spikenard very precious; and she brake the box and poured it on His head (Mark 14:3).

Have you ever wondered why this woman did not choose to dab only a small amount of the fragrant ointment on Jesus?

After all, this ointment was rare and costly. Spikenard was an ointment imported from India. One jar (in ancient times) would have cost the equivalent of a worker's annual income. This was more than a token gesture; this was a sacrificial offering.

The woman was Mary of Bethany, the sister of Martha and Lazarus. She is mentioned in the gospels three times, and each time, she is found at the feet of Jesus. Mary knew real worship.

It was six days before Passover and the city was crowded with people. Based on the events of the previous days, Mary's house was filled with excitement and awe. Jesus had just raised her brother, Lazarus, from the dead, and word in that arid land had traveled fast. Folks knew about the special relationship between Jesus and this family. When Jesus came to Bethany, this was the house where He often stayed; these people were his friends. This occasion was special, though, with a dual meaning. Mary and Martha had planned a dinner to celebrate the miracle of their brother Lazarus's resurrection from the dead. It was to be a final meal for Jesus, with those whom He considered family.

A trial, a cross, and a tomb would lay ahead for Mary's friend. Mary did not come to this dinner to make a request to Jesus, or to fellowship with other people. She was not there with an "event" mindset. She was there with spiritual anticipation of His death; and she prepared His body in a public ceremony.

A Fragrant Gift of Worship

The highest purpose of worship is for God, not for us, which Mary demonstrated by her actions and her offering. Mary did not just use a portion of ointment to anoint Jesus. She did not try to keep any of it for her own purposes; instead, she broke the box and poured out all the ointment, eliminating any possibility of saving some for another occasion.

Many in the Church worship the Lord with restrictions and reservations. They make a great demonstration of presenting their token gifts, but keep the greater part of their lives—their hearts—for themselves. They may give an hour or two to God each week, but the rest belongs to them. Others may give a small percentage of their income, but retain ownership of the rest. Too often people offer a portion of their talents and gifts in God's service, but the greater part is expended in lives devoted to self-interest.

Such people know little about true worship and have limited understanding concerning the lordship of Jesus Christ. Jesus uses broken vessels.

A broken vessel can no longer retain its contents. It is powerless to withhold; therefore, it freely spills out all that is within. This is the purpose of the breaking. When we are experiencing the breaking process and have pain, it does not bring pleasure to God. No! The pain is part of the process, but it is not the single purpose. The goal is the fragrance, the sweet aroma that fills the air...and the nostrils of God.

Although Mary was hosting many, she was a worshiper of the One, and her actions alone transformed the dinner into a worship service. Those in the room rejected her worship, but she did not allow rejection to dictate her response (worship) to Jesus. The fragrance of her gift brought all the attention to Him. She wiped His feet with her hair, which for a woman signifies her glory and identity. She invested herself in worship to Christ, bowing low to lift Him high.

The spikenard, her gift that day, also represents the essence of the contents of our hearts. Our minds, wills, and emotions are the ingredients that make the fragrance of life so valuable, the same fragrance which filled the room. But the earthen jar had to first be broken and poured out.

We must be willing to break the box around our hearts to release our praise unto God. Many worship inside the boxes of religion, pride, religious personalities, or musical styles. Only through allowing this process, and offering the pure love of a broken life, will we become the "anointed fragrance of worship" by which we can adorn our Savior. And yes, it is a response to the fragrance filled atmosphere.

We are called to ministry, but created to worship. True worship is birthed, cultivated, and maintained through a relationship with the King.

The Atmosphere of Intimacy

During a worship service, if we are not careful, we can place our focus on our problems, people, etc. When we do this, we are placing our attention on someone or something other than God. When we focus our attention on the wrong things, we are actually worshiping them. When His presence is there, we are bowing to other things.

The first six months of Esther's preparation speaks of cleansing and purification. If we want to live in God's presence, we must make repentance part of our daily routine. *"Enter into His gates with **thanksgiving*** *and into His courts with **praise**. Be thankful to Him and bless His name"* (Ps. 100:4 NKJV).

Thanksgiving is fundamental to bringing us into His presence. However, there is more. We must enter His inner courts of the palace with praise. There is a difference between thanksgiving and praise. We thank God because He has done something for us. We praise Him because of *who* He is.

Worship is different from praise in the sense that our lives become the praise offered to Him. The only thing necessary to qualify us to praise Him is breath. However, to know Him intimately takes worship.

He is worthy of worship simply because *He is!*

It takes a pure heart to worship God just because *He is,* and not because we want or received something. The sincerity of worship takes priority over the method or ability of how we worship.

Many pass the gates of thanksgiving and enter the courts of praise, but it is rare to enter the place of *intimacy* reserved for true worshipers. The deeper you go into the palace, the fewer people remain. Only those with a true relationship with God enter into the inner chambers.

Endnote

1. *Matthew Henry Commentary on the Whole Bible*, Esther http://www.ccel.org/ccel/henry/mhc.i.html.

Points to Ponder

1. Do you more often leave church feeling blessed or that you have blessed God?

_____

_____

_____

_____

2. Have you experienced the fragrance of God? Describe it.

_____

_____

_____

_____

6

Healing Worship

WHEN WE ENTER THE INNER chamber in worship, His presence will manifest and make provision for what we need. It is at that moment, we make a great exchange. We give him our worship and He gives us His presence. Whatever we need, He supplies. If we need a healing, we offer an offering of praise and He responds with His offering of grace. Mercy extends from Heaven and the balm of Gilead supplies healing through the blood of Christ.

Let's explore the biblical story of the woman with the issue of blood. The great multitude followed Him and thronged Him; but a certain woman had a flow of blood for twelve years. She had been to every physician and consumed every form of medicine or potion made available in those days. After twelve long years of misery, she was desperate and wanted to be healed. She may have been a rich woman originally, but every last coin had been exhausted on wasted efforts to make her whole again. (See Matthew 9:19-22.)

I can only imagine the scale of emotion this woman went through… from sorrow and despair, to bitterness and anger. She had done all she could do in her own strength, to no avail.

But one day as she lurked at the edge of the village afraid to mingle with the people, she overheard talk of a prophet named Jesus. He healed people! Could this be possible? Was there a chance for her to be healed? Then her heart sank when she realized that she couldn't get near Him because of her condition, her "uncleanness." It was not acceptable in her culture for a woman to speak to a man in public, unless he was her husband.

So she went about her life, but could not forget what she had heard about this Jesus. Then one day there was an unusual excitement in town. Crowds were everywhere. Jesus had come! Her heart started beating faster…what did she have to lose? She had already lost everything. Even death would be a relief.

Pulling her covering far over her head, she slowly made her way to the town. No one noticed her. Everyone's focus was upon the prophet. With her head down, she moved among the crowd, afraid to raise her eyes. It had been so long since she had been so close to any people at all, except for physicians. She hardly breathed in her excitement, but continued to press forward. Suddenly, there was a break in the crowd. There was Jesus! He looked like any other man. His disciples stood near to keep the people from pressing Him, but still they crowded around Him. A man was on his knees before Jesus, crying in desperation, something about his sick daughter.

Without hesitation, the woman fell to her knees and crawled as fast as she could, pushing through the people. She had to get to Him, not caring what people thought, or what they might do. All she knew was that she had to touch Him! With all her heart, she believed if she could just touch Him, she would be made whole. It was her only hope, her last chance. Time stood still as she reached toward the hem of His garment. The crowd was pushing her to the side, but with all that she had in her, she grasped His hem, she simultaneously felt a rush of power course through her. An incredible sense of peace ensued. She knew she had been healed! Letting go of His garment, she covered her face as tears streamed down her cheeks.

"*Who touched me?*" asked a strong voice from above her. (See Luke 8:45.)

She remained on the ground, head buried in her hands, fearful of what might happen next. But she couldn't resist gazing into the kind eyes of the man who had just made her whole. She told Him her story of twelve years of illness; the desperation, the despair, the hopelessness—until He came along, and her hope was restored.

He smiled gently, took her by the hand, and raised her to her feet, "*Daughter, be of good comfort: thy faith hath made thee whole; go in peace*" (Luke 8:48).

Three Levels to Healing

Notice the levels she went through to receive her healing:

Level One. There was a multitude (the crowd). The masses made it difficult for her to see where Jesus was. She would have had to listen through the commotion to discover His whereabouts.

There will always be distractions that will prevent us from seeing our way out of our current situation and finding the place of miracles. The atmosphere can be overwhelming, but we must press beyond the crowds.

Level Two. There were a few within the crowd who were in the immediate vicinity of Jesus, those who thronged Him. At this level, she would have been closer, but the reactions of those who were close would physically prevent her from touching Him.

To get past the onlookers was one thing, but to get beyond the compact crowd was quite another. The place of His presence is not reserved for those who are special or elite. We may feel frustrated or inadequate, but God is no respecter of persons. She humbled herself and crawled to Him.

Level Three. There was only *one* who touched Him, not just in the natural, but Spirit to spirit. Even the disciples were baffled at Jesus' statement, *"Who touched me?"*, for the crowds were grabbing Him and pulling Him every direction. This woman touched Him with *faith*.

Pressing through the commotion (crowds and chaos) are Levels One and Two; however, if we pursue Him for any other reason but to connect our faith, it will be in vain. Many touched Him that day, but only one from the heart. Her action was worship. She desired to be close to Him, knowing she would not be rejected. Remember, God is the One who invites us to come. We must approach Him with faith, knowing we are welcome. With the right motive, when we worship Him, we will receive what we need.

Kissing God With Worship

The most common word for worship in the New Testament is *pro-skun-e-o,* which occurs over 60 times, and literally means, "to come forward to kiss"[1] God is love, and the whole point of worship is that God desires His people to respond to Him in love. When we "come forward to kiss," to show our love for God by opening ourselves to

Him in worship, then we are, in turn, able to receive even more of His love, poured into our hearts by the Holy Spirit (see Rom 5:5). By contrast, worship without that intimate relationship of love is just empty and worthless.

I find it interesting that "worship" is translated, "toward" and "kiss," or to kiss toward. We have the expression in America "to kiss up to," usually in reference to our boss at work. Although this phrase has a negative connotation, we can still draw lessons from it. One who "kisses up" is generally thought to be someone who is trying to get ahead and is willing to go to great lengths to win the boss's favor, and hopefully receive a raise and promotion. The person ingratiates himself or herself with the boss through flattery, and by being available to carry out every whim of the boss, no matter how silly or demeaning. The person at heart may not respect the boss at all, and may even resent him or her, but is willing to "play the game" to achieve the desired end.

Despite these negative connotations, we may expound upon some themes. Obviously, God does not want us to just go through the motions to appease Him in some fashion or to make points with Him. On the one hand, we have nothing to offer, and on the other, He does not need us to flatter His ego. He wants a relationship with us. He wants us to love Him because He has already loved us.

Instead of hollow flattery or lip service, He wants us to worship in Spirit and in truth. Instead of doing one thing in His presence in assembly, and another when away, He wants us to do His will, whether in assembly or by ourselves. And performing His will springs forth from our heart and not in outward behavior alone.

Obedience is better than sacrifice, God says. He likes honest worship; honesty, which flows from love and a life lived pleasing Him. The thought of "kissing toward" is something like blowing God kisses with our words and ways. Kissing is one of the most tender expressions of love we can make—a kiss offered to Him is an expression of tender love toward our Lord. God desires to be kissed! The Bible says in Psalm 2:12, *"Kiss the Son, lest He be angry...."*

Not every kiss is a kiss of worship. Judas kissed Jesus with the wrong motive and it cost his life. Some people may kiss Him and worship Him, but others may kiss Him with a kiss of betrayal.

Worship the King

Isaiah saw the Lord on a throne, high and lifted up, with His train filling the Temple (God's house or palace on earth). The seraphs, His shining angelic retainers, worship, *"Holy, holy, holy, is the Lord Almighty; the whole earth is full of His glory."* Isaiah was staggered: *"Woe to me."* He was a man of unclean lips. *"My eyes have seen the King, the Lord Almighty"* (see Isa. 6:1-5 NIV).

Micaiah revealed the Lord, *"sitting on His throne with all the host of heaven standing around Him on His right and on His left"* (1 Kings 22:19). Ezekiel's heavenly vision included a throne with a burning, divine figure on it. When he saw it, he fell face down (see Ezek. 1:26-28) For Daniel, God sat on a fiery throne, giving an everlasting kingdom to the Son of Man (see Dan. 7:9-10;13-14). In the New Testament, John was transported into Heaven before the Creator's throne, where angels worship (see Rev. 4:1-11).

In the Psalms, God is proclaimed King: *"...the Lord is the great God, the great King above all gods"* (Ps. 95:3 NKJV). He sits on his throne: *"The Lord reigns, let the nations tremble; He sits enthroned..."* (Ps. 99:1 NIV). His garments are regal: *"The Lord reigns, He is robed in* majesty; the Lord is robed in majesty and is armed with strength…" (Ps. 93:1 NIV). A footstool stands below His throne: *"Exalt the Lord our God and worship at His footstool; He is holy"* (Ps. 99:5 NIV). He holds a scepter in His hand: *"Your throne, O God, will last for ever and ever; a scepter of justice will be the scepter of Your kingdom"* (Ps. 45:6 NIV). He is surrounded with heavenly retainers: *"…He sits enthroned between the cherubim, let the earth shake"* (Ps. 99:1). He is worshiped by a sea of angels: *"Praise the Lord, you His angels…Praise the Lord, all His heavenly host"* (Ps. 103:20-21).

In what ways do we worship the King? We have discussed how our thoughts, ways, and words should be all for God. In this sense, all that we do is worship, *"whatsoever ye do, do all to the glory of God."* There are also those special times, however, when we are specifically setting aside time to worship God. We may do this individually, during our quiet times of meditation and prayer, and at other times, when we worship together with other Christians. It is a special time when we get to come into the presence of God Himself as a company of believers and worship. This is a special privilege that Old Testament saints were not able to enjoy.

Worship Then and Now

Old Testament believers worshiped God by bringing their sacrifices to the Temple at Jerusalem. The people themselves could not offer the sacrifices, much less come into the presence of God. Only the priests could offer the sacrifices, and come into the holy place. Even then, only the high priest was allowed into the holiest of holies, just once a year.

Today, every believer is a priest and is able to come into the presence of God; no go-between is necessary, and there is no veil separating

God from His people. All have equal access and privilege to Him. No longer is there only one physical place to meet God, as Jerusalem was in the Old Testament. Now He is wherever two or three are gathered in His name. The church is the Temple of God, His dwelling place on earth, and it is only corporately that we can enjoy the privilege of being in His presence to worship in this special way. The Temple in Jerusalem was the preeminent place for worship in the Old Testament, and today, His Temple is the church.

In ancient times, worshipers brought sacrifices such as doves, lambs, and bullocks. Today we worship in Spirit and in truth, and bring our sacrifice of praise, which is the fruit of our lips. For us, Christ is the Lamb of God who takes away our sins. He is a sweet savor to God, and when we gather to worship, we simply bring what He is and what He has done for us. No more sacrifice is necessary.

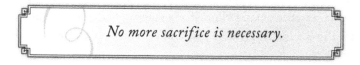

No more sacrifice is necessary.

In biblical times, even the poorest in Israel could worship. God made provision that if one could not afford a lamb, he could offer two doves. If the person offering the sacrifice could not afford two doves, he could offer fine flour. God is pleased with whatever we have to offer if our offering is done with the proper heart. Even the spiritually poor may worship God; remember, He was more pleased with two mites from the widow than with all the treasures offered by the rich.

"Out of the mouth of babes and sucklings thou hast perfected praise" (Matt. 21:16). If you can make nothing more than the feeblest sacrifice, God is pleased, for anything that speaks of His Son is pleasing to Him.

Two types of people served at the Temple at Jerusalem: Levites and priests. The Levite tribe was specifically designated by God to serve in the things of the Temple, but did not offer sacrifices. The priests were Levites of Aaron's family only, with the special privilege of serving in the Temple and offering sacrifices for the people. The priests actually carried out the sacrifices. It was the priests only who could enter into the presence of the Lord. This illustrates the difference between worship and service, although they are, in some ways, inseparable.

Thank God, that He has made all Christians priests! Let's not confuse our special privileges as priests with service. While service is wonderful, necessary, and pleasing to the Lord, our highest privilege as priests is that we can enter into God's presence for worship, bringing praise to His name. Preaching and teaching are excellent, as well as evangelism, and every other form of service, but this is not worshiping.

Worship is bringing the sweet savor of Christ up to God in praise. Worship is not possible without Levitical service, but it is not Levitical service that constitutes worship in His presence. The Lord specifically asks us to gather to remember Him in His death. The Father seeks worshipers—let's heed the call.

In Hebrew, the word *worship* [shakah] means to fall down or bow down: *"Come, let us bow down in worship, let us kneel before the Lord our Maker; for He is our God…"* (Ps. 95:6-7 NIV). To fall down is to surrender, to give up, becoming physically lower than the King. It is humbling. We are helpless, at the Sovereign's mercy. This is where worship begins. It destroys our narcissistic "What's in it for me?" attitude. Worship is not getting; it is giving. We give our lives over to God. To withhold is to revolt. To surrender is to worship: *"The sacrifices of God are a broken spirit; a broken and contrite heart, O God, you will not despise"* (Ps. 51:17 NIV).

The Christian life begins with worship (submission) and confession: Jesus is Lord! (see Rom. 10:9). Paul says to offer our bodies as living sacrifices, this is our spiritual act of worship (see Rom. 12:1). It is holistic and intentional. When we lay our body down before God, He has us.

Second, God taught Israel never to come to Him empty handed. Just as heads of state honor each other with gifts, so we bring our gifts to God. We bring the gift of ourselves. We bring the gift of our praise. We sing to Him; we shout to Him, a ringing cry of victory: *"Shout for joy to the Lord, all the earth. Worship the Lord with gladness; come before Him with joyful songs"* (Ps. 100:1-2 NIV). We honor and extol Him as the object of our worship. This expresses loving Him with all our heart. We tell of His greatness, His goodness, and His faithfulness. We marvel over His character and His works. Here, worship turns into witness. We remember God's mighty deeds. We recall His miracles, His deliverance from Egypt, His rescue from the hands of the enemy, His forgiving our sins, His healings, and His triumph over death. As we proclaim His mighty deeds, the nations listen. They come to fear and honor the one true God:

> *Sing to the Lord, praise His name; proclaim His salvation day after day. Declare His glory among the nations, His marvelous deeds among all peoples* (Psalm 96:2-3 NIV).

As we worship, we also bring our gifts, our sacrifices, our tithes, and our offerings. We pay our vows. These are acts of obedience. They maintain the Temple and its priesthood. They are also acts of love and devotion as we give God His due:

> *Sacrifice thank offerings to God, fulfill your vows to the Most High* (Psalm 50:14 NIV).

Third, worship includes petition. Dallas Willard says that requests are the heart of prayer. We bring them to the Great King, approaching boldly the throne of God as sons and daughters. As we petition, we come on our behalf, and on the behalf of others, representing those who do not know the King. In their idolatry and unbelief, they cannot come themselves. We lay out our requests, knowing that God's face is turned toward us. He is anxious to receive them and to answer them for our good and His glory.

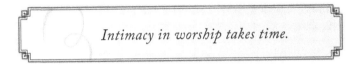

Intimacy in worship takes time.

Achieving Intimacy

How, then, do we achieve intimacy in worship without making people cringe or bolt for the door?

The first thing to understand is the balance between what is appropriate in public, and what is best kept private. It is a difficult balance. We know from the Gospels that Jesus did not despise or shun public worship. He was often found in synagogues or the Temple, teaching people about the Kingdom of God in large, public gatherings. But Jesus does suggest, in Matthew chapter 6, that our most intimate experiences of prayer will be in private, behind closed doors, totally alone with God, or perhaps with a small, intimate group—not in a crowd.

Isn't that true of all intimacy? The lover and the beloved need to be alone together, as a worshiper needs to be in solitude with God. Public gatherings for worship are important, of course. However, they are no substitute for the intimacy with God that can only be discovered and nurtured in private.

The second thing about intimacy in worship is that it takes time. You do not go into your room and shut the door only to rush off again a few moments later. Go to your room, take a walk in the forest, hike the hills, or plod to the center of your garden—go somewhere you can find privacy, and be alone with God. Constant busyness kills intimacy and prevents us from becoming still in God's presence, to receive, and respond to His love.

If I get too busy with life in general or even with ministry, it hinders me from hearing God's voice. Then I begin to get frustrated and make poor decisions. Just because I'm in ministry doesn't mean I don't have to have time alone with God. I feel I need it more because hundreds and sometimes, thousands of people who I minister to need to hear a fresh word from God. Without His revelation, I will not know how the Father wants me to minister. I depend upon His voice to guide me.

Staying too busy stops a clear communication between God and me. It hinders my spiritual senses if I block my heavenly connection with "other things" as God spoke of in Psalm 27:4, "*One* thing I desire" not *other* things.

Third, to create some space and make some time for the privacy and solitude that intimacy in worship requires, other things must be eliminated. That is the point of fasting. Priorities need to be reordered, clearing away the clutter. We need to spend less time preparing elaborate meals and consuming rich food and drink, or in diversions like watching television or reading magazines, or whatever occupies large chunks of our time and attention. It requires cutting down and fasting from them for a period of time.

Sometimes, Pamela and I feel the need to fast from television for a period of time. We call the cable company to suspend our services for a period. During these fasts, it gives us more available time to spend with God. It gives us the opportunity to recalibrate our life. It also creates more family time, building a stronger relationship between each family member.

Jesus was aware that some religious people used fasting—as they used everything else in their lives—merely to "show off." Therefore, He reminds His followers that real intimacy in worship is not like that at all. It is not about an outward show, it is not a public display of the most intimate secrets that should stay where they belong—between God and you.

Finally, and above all, intimacy in worship is about attitude. It is about our mindset and where our heart truly is. Jesus says, *"For where your treasure is, there your heart will be also"* (Matt. 6:21). Lovers know this. Lovers have their hearts and minds set upon their beloved, the person whom they most want to be with, the one whose company and presence they enjoy the most. If our attitude toward God really is that we long for His divine love to come down upon us whenever we worship, then He will indeed draw nearer and nearer to us. If we mean what we say when we sing praise and worship songs unto Him, "I love You more than any other, so much more than anything," or if we at least *want* to mean it (even though our hearts might feel cold and numb), then God will see that attitude of openness and obedience. And our Father, who sees what is done in the secret places of the heart, will reward us with the gift of His intimate presence.

Endnote

1. *Wycliffe Bible Dictionary.*

Points to Ponder

1. What is worship?

_____

_____

_____

_____

2. What is the fragrance of worship?

_____

_____

_____

_____

3. How can you create an atmosphere for intimacy with God?

7

The Love of God

*L*OVE IS A MYSTERY, AND yet is the most important thing in the world. It is so important that *love* is used 808 times in the Bible. Love is expressed and evident throughout God's creation—in flowers, trees, animals, and the stars. Each one of His creations speaks, "I love you...I created these things just for you to enjoy, because I love you." Unfortunately, many take His love for granted.

One day as I was sitting alone in my living room, I asked God to teach me His love—I wanted to *know* His love, not know *about* it. God spoke to me and said, "This is the channel that you can find Me on... the Love Channel." We need to "dial in to" God's love to experience and hear Him.

Love is the only thing that will unite you with the Father. Humankind was created by love to answer the heart cry of the Father, fellowship with Him. Outside of God's love, humanity is a failure.

*"If a man loves Me, He will keep My words: and My Father will love him, and **We** will come unto him and make Our abode with him"* (John 14:23).

We love Him, because He first loved us (1 John 4:19).

Unless you experience the love of God for yourself, you cannot love God or others with this depth of love. We are not originators of this God-kind of love. We have to receive it first. We must know it experientially, and then we can give it out.

We experience healing from God as we realize that in Christ, God truly accepts us. He does not love us stoically, "grinning and bearing us." He actually likes us! And with our sins taken away through the atonement of Christ, God has genuine pleasure in us. He loves us. He wants us to respond to His love.

It is a work of the Holy Spirit to reveal God's love. *"The love of God has been poured out in our hearts by the Holy Spirit who was given to us"* (Rom. 5:5 NKJV). We cannot achieve this knowledge of God by striving in our flesh. We have to be willing at some point just to "open our hearts" and receive it. What hinders us is hardened hearts, crusted over by layers of pride, cynicism, anger, selfishness, and un-belief. This often happens without our conscious awareness. I know from my own experience.

I got hurt so many times by others in ministry (which created an-ger); it caused me to begin to close my heart and prevent others to get close to me. I didn't want to get hurt again. The more I did that, the harder my heart became. I didn't realize it was affecting my compassion and love for others. God begin to deal with me, and I surrendered to the King; and the layers that I had built up came off.

It takes a work of God to soften a hard heart. It takes a work of God to heal a heart that has been hurt by rejection over the years. God wants to do this for you, and *He will,* if you yield to His love. If you want to know God's love for you, do not try in your own strength. Instead, just talk honestly with God. Talk out loud, and tell Him how you feel. Invite Him to work in your life and then be prepared to wait. It may not happen immediately, because He may be talking to you about first forgiving others. Respond to what He shows you; in time, He will reveal His love to you personally.

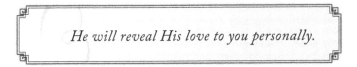

He will reveal His love to you personally.

When you separate yourself from love, you separate yourself from God. To walk in love is actually to live in God. When we step out of love, we step out of the *will* of the Master.

The name of Jesus gives us access to the Father; but if we step out of love, His name is of no value to us. We can only use the name of Jesus as we walk in love. Some prayers may go unanswered if we step out of love. The love of God is a divine encounter.

> *May Christ through your faith [actually] dwell (settle down, abide, make His permanent home) in your hearts! May you be rooted deep in love and founded securely on love. That you may have the power and be strong to apprehend and grasp with all the saints [God's devoted people, the experience of that love] what is the breadth and length and height and depth [of it]; [That you may really come] to know [practically, through experience for yourselves] the love of Christ, which far surpasses*

mere knowledge [without experience]; that you may be filled [through all your being] unto all the fullness of God [may have the richest measure of the divine Presence, and become a body wholly filled and flooded with God Himself]! Now to Him Who, by (in consequence of) the [action of His] power that is at work within us, is able to [carry out His purpose and] do superabundantly, far over and above all that we [dare] ask or think [infinitely beyond our highest prayers, desires, thoughts, hopes, or dreams] (Ephesians 3:17-20 AMP).

An encounter with God's love is transforming. We cannot substitute God for religion, because religion is not an encounter. A God-encounter negates religion. A God-encounter will take you past "knowledge." A person does not have to experience what I experience, but he or she does have to experience God to understand love.

Love will transform us in the workplace, at the office, in our home, or at school. Love never takes advantage of anyone. Love always bears the burden of the weak. Love says, "It's my fault, dear. If I was walking in love, it never would have happened." There will be no divorce when a husband and wife are walking in God's love.

This kind of love is not an option. A life that manifests *no* love for others is a life in which the seed of God is not germinating. The basic motivations of such a person are wrong. A person whose principle motivation is fame, feeds his pride satisfying fleshly longings, or desires to acquire more material things, is a person walking in the flesh. Such people, whether they claim to be a "born-again Christian" or not, are on the path that leads to destruction (see Rom. 8:5-6).

...those who live like this shall not inherit the kingdom of God (Galatians 5:21 NIV).

Do not love the world or the things in the world. If anyone loves the world, the love of the Father is not in him (1 John 2:15 NKJV).

The Fruit of Love

It is one thing to know that God demands the fruit of love from us, but how is it accomplished?

The first step to walking in the love of God is to be born again and receive a new nature from Him. This step is vital. If you are not born again, you can be right now, simply by calling upon the name of Jesus, asking Him to save you and make you a new person—trusting in His sacrifice of Himself for you, and His resurrection—and giving your life to Him.

Once born again, we still need to be transformed before we are really walking in love. The programming of our brain does not cause us to react in love. Rather, until our minds and hearts are renewed, we may act with the same kind of irritability, selfishness, pride, anger, envy, and faithlessness in certain situations that "press our buttons." There is an ongoing process of *sanctification*, which we must embrace if we are going to walk in love as God requires. Although our spirits are made new when we are born again, our minds are not and require renewal by an application of the Word of God into our lives.

The Mark of a Genuine Christian

A.W. Tozer felt that a genuine Christian would stand out in the world because he or she is connected to God. He felt that if today's Christian is genuine, he is "separated," much like the Romans isolated the Jews:

The Christian, the genuine Christian, realizes that he is indeed a lonely soul in the middle of a world which affords him no fellowship. I contend that if the Christian breaks down on occasion and goes in tears, he ought not to feel that he is weak. It is a normal loneliness in the midst of a world that has disowned him. He has to be a lonely man!

Those to whom Peter wrote were strangers in many ways, first of all because they were Jews. They were Jews scattered among the Romans and they never could accept and bow to the Roman ways. They learned the Greek tongue in the world of their day, but they never could learn the Roman ways. They were Jews, a people apart, even as they are today.

Besides that, they had become Christian believers, so they were no longer merely Jews. Their sense of alienation from the world around them had increased and doubled. They were not only Jews—unlike the Gentiles around them—but they were Christians, unlike the Jews as well as unlike the Gentiles!

This is the reason that it is easily possible for a Christian believer to be the loneliest person in the world under a set of certain circumstances. This sense of not belonging is a part of our Christian heritage. That sense of belonging in another world and not belonging to this one steals into the Christian bosom and marks him off as being different from the people around him. Many of our hymns have been born out of that very loneliness, that sense of another and higher citizenship![1]

The Bible says, *"Love your neighbor"* (Lev. 19:18 NKJV). Our neighbor is anybody nearby us, no matter where we might be.

A new commandment I give unto you that you love one another; as I loved you, that you also love one another. By this all will know that you are My disciples, if you have love for one another (John 13:34-35 NKJV).

Speaking in tongues, preaching a sermon, or laying hands on the sick does not prove we are true Christians. But love does. When we walk in God's love, people will know that we have been with Jesus, just like the disciples.

I have heard preachers say, "Well, my job is to preach the truth, but it's not my problem whether they receive it or not." However, Ephesians 4:15 says, *"Instead, speaking the truth **in love**, we will in all things grow up into Him who is the Head, that is, Christ"* (NIV).

It is not what they hear (providing it is within the context of the Word); it is what they receive. Love is what makes the Word receivable. The love of God leads people to salvation and into transformation. The love of God brings us to an encounter.

Love Is the Key

An attitude of selfishness will destroy our spirit and prevent us from walking in God's love. Selfishness is the outlaw seeking to exalt self. Love is its adversary. Selfishness seeks to dethrone the love of God in our hearts, and is a robber and a thief. It makes men dissemble. It breaks friendships, wrecks homes, and ruins churches.

The Scriptures say, *"And because iniquity shall abound, the love of many shall wax cold"* (Matt. 24:12). The moment a church leaves the love realm, satan gains accessibility. The love of God has adhesive power, which binds us together. It is difficult to love hypocrites or our enemies, but if Jesus did it, so can we. The same Spirit that raised

Jesus from the dead dwells in our mortal body. Through the Holy Spirit, we can even love a Judas or a Pharisee.

Our measuring stick of love is Jesus. The Master loved the man that drove the nails into Jesus' hands. On the cross, He cried out to Heaven, *"Father, forgive them; for they know not what they do"* (Luke 23:34). That is LOVE!

> Because he has set his love upon Me therefore I will deliver him; I will set him on high because he has known My name. He shall call upon Me, and I will answer him; I will be with him in trouble I will deliver him and honor him. With long life I will satisfy him and show him My salvation (Psalm 91:14-16 NKJV).

Love Versus Fear

Since September 11, 2001, terrorism has taken a new meaning in the United States, and throughout the world. Terrorism is the planned, organized use of fear as a weapon in order to scare or paralyze its victims to the point where they cannot resist oppression.

America has many enemies, and as long as we are subject to the possibility of harm through terrorism, fear is inevitable. The effort to conquer fear without recognizing the root is altogether futile. As long as we rely entirely on our resources for survival, and our ability to out-think or out-maneuver the enemy, we have good reason to be afraid. And fear hath torment.

But to know that love is of God, and to enter into the secret place, leaning upon the arm of the King, this, and only this, can cast out fear. Let a man become convinced that nothing can harm him, and fear departs. "The nervous reflex, the natural revulsion to physical pain, may be felt sometimes, but the deep torment of fear is gone forever."[2]

However, in the daily life of a person in the United States, the real weapon of terrorism is not in bombs, guns, chemicals, or hijacked planes—it is fear! If you remove fear, you remove the only real weapon satan has. We are not to control fear, but rather eradicate it from our lives.

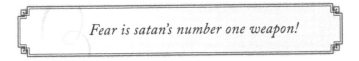

Fear is satan's number one weapon!

There is actually a Website called phobialist.com that lists alphabetically all the types of phobias that people suffer from. Under the letter A alone, there are 79 listings. Some of them are well-known such as: apiphobia, the fear of bees; aviophobia or aviatophobia, the fear of flying; and arachnephobia or arachnophobia, the fear of spiders. And others seem foolish: alliumphobia, the fear of garlic, arachibutyrophobia, the fear of peanut butter sticking to the roof of the mouth, and aulophobia, the fear of flutes.

But for most people, fear is very real and, unfortunately, part of their daily lives. They are gripped with haunting thoughts that paralyze them from attaining their potential in life and with God. Most commonly: fear of death, the root of all fear; fear of what people think; fear of financial lack; fear of failure; fear of change; and, fear to be loved or to love.

First John 4:18 says, *"Perfect love casteth out fear."* Our love relationship with God reveals His nature. If we really know God, we would not worry; but if we are insecure in our relationship with God, we are governed by fear. The Bible says, *"God has not given us the spirit of fear but of power, love, and a sound mind,"* (2 Tim. 1:7 NKJV). A lack of power, love, and a "sound mind" will cause a person to live in fear.

David was gripped with fear when Uzzah was killed when he touched the Ark of the Covenant. David, and those with him, refused to carry the ark any farther (see 2 Sam. 6:6-10). The power of fear prevented them from reaching their destiny. Sidney B. Simon explains the dangers of fear and how it can cripple our faith:[3]

1. Fear persuades you to lower your goals, minimizing your success and reward.

2. Fear triggers internal defense systems, establishing frail excuses as unchangeable to avoid the effort of change.

3. Fear of failure or disappointment decapitates viable options and destroys alternatives, keeping you from pursuing them.

4. Fear causes indecisiveness and confusion, thwarting the risk required for new experiences and relationships.

5. Fear warps self-perception and robs the joy intended for your life.

6. Fear blocks seeking help when you need it and from benefiting from others' emotional support.

7. Fear keeps you from asserting yourself, locking you into a pervading prison of mediocrity.

8. Fear forces unhealthy habits and behavior in search for relief.

9. Fear holds the capacity of stopping you just one step short of your goal.

10. Fear keeps you from taking risks.

Our authority and security lies in the love of God. You may be wondering what possible connection is there between God's love and no fear? When fear arises in an area of life:

- Most people actually yield to it.

- Some people say, "I have to attack it."

- Some have deficiency of love (in that area).

- You need to replace it with love.

What if you were diagnosed with a terminal disease and you were tempted to *fear*. Some would say, "You need to build your faith up." Yes, this is true, but how do you do that when facing a difficult time? Faith or confidence is built upon the revelation of God. The more you know Him, the easier it is to trust Him. You cannot wait until you get a bad report to "build up" your love relationship with God. You must build up your faith every day.

The apostle Paul said, *"Therefore we do not lose heart. Though outwardly we are wasting away, yet inwardly we are being renewed day by day"* (2 Cor. 4:16 NIV).

The Bible says, *"Faith cometh by hearing and hearing by the word of God,"* but without love, it is impossible to demonstrate faith (Rom. 10:17). I once heard a minister say, "Fear that is tolerated contaminates your faith." I agree.

God is love, and in love, there is no fear—not an ounce! Fear is a spiritual force. Love is a spiritual force. For fear to enter into the heart of a believer, it must come from the outside, and not inside-out. Fear is the spiritual connector to disaster and death.

Entering the Kingdom

When we are walking in love, we demonstrate His Kingdom. It is our heavenly right as a citizen of the Kingdom to manifest love.

> *[The Father] has delivered and drawn us to Himself out of the control and dominion of darkness and has transferred us into the kingdom of the Son of His Love* (Colossians 1:13 AMP).

> *As the Father hath loved me, so have I loved you: continue ye in My love. If ye keep My commandments, ye shall abide in My love; even as I have kept my Father's commandments, and abide in His love* (John 15:9-10).

We are to be permanent inhabitants of the realm of love as His sons and daughters, because love governs His Kingdom. As we become ambassadors of love, we make an impact in the world.

God instructed me *not* to teach *love* like it is just another topic. I commonly teach on subjects of faith, joy, and prosperity. They are essential topics, but *love* is the foundation for everything He is and does.

Without love, there is no redemption, no healing, and no you! Everything stems from love. If we do not see things through love, then we cannot perceive things as God sees them. If we do not "present" all that we do through love, we are not doing it by the Spirit of God.

Even *giving* is an act of love. It is not the amount or the finances that qualifies the spirit of giving. It is love. Giving is love in action!

What we do with our money is a reflection of the condition of our hearts. If we truly are walking in God's love, then no one needs to tell or ask us to give.

The two ultimate acts of giving:

1. God gave His only Son for us.

2. God's Son gave His life for us.

Love puts a heavenly fragrance into our giving and fills the heart of the receiver with joy. Giving is obedience in its truest form. We must be obedient to love. Sowing a seed in love will change our future.

"Seeking" is an act of love. If we seek His face and gaze into His eyes, we will discover the highest degree of love. Matthew says, *"But seek ye first the kingdom of God* [love] *and His righteousness; and all these things shall be added unto you"* (Matt. 6:33). We cannot enter the Kingdom without discovering the meaning of love. Without love, we will never experience true joy. Romancing the King is based upon love— love is the key, and Jesus is our example.

Endnotes

1. "The genuine Christian is a lonely soul" by A.W. Tozer. http://missionxp. webblogg.se/190206142249_the_genuine_christian_ is_a_lonel.html.

2. http://evanlenz.net/blog/2004/11/01/perfect-love-drives-out-fear/; A.W. Tozer, *The Knowledge of the Holy.*

3. Sidney B. Simon, *Getting Unstuck: Breaking Through Your Barriers to Change,* (New York, NY: Warner Books, Inc.. 1988); http://www. depression.oldguy.us/fear.php.

Points to Ponder

The Love of a King:

1. How do you define love?

_____

_____

_____

_____

2. How do you enter the Kingdom of God?

_____

_____

_____

_____

8

The Friendship of the Holy Spirit

I HAVE BEEN ON A QUEST to understand the love of God for several years. In the previous chapter, we learned the meaning of God's love. But in order to experience the love of God, we need to know the Holy Spirit. He is the Agent through whom we fellowship with God. The Holy Spirit is God, and He is the Person of the Godhead who reveals His nature to us. There is no competition within the Trinity.

Unfortunately, I believe many people in church who are filled with the Holy Spirit are drawing back from Him. Could it be that some churches are more interested in church attendance than the power and demonstration of the Holy Spirit? Have churches become duplexes where we divide up His house and put the Holy Spirit in the back room because if He moves, the people might leave the church?

James 4:8 says, *"Draw near to God and He will draw near to you."* We cannot withdraw from the Holy Spirit and be close to God because

He is the Agent through whom we know God. The Spirit is probably the least talked about Person in the Trinity within the Church. Why does He take the back seat?

We are to pray to the Father in Jesus' name, but all that we do is through the Holy Spirit. Do we see Him as a Person or a presence? Is the third Person of the Godhead a forgotten figure in Christianity today?

It is important that we know who He is, why He was sent, and His office. I am concerned that Christians today are living below their God-intended potential and are missing the blessings and benefits that the Holy Spirit came to give.

Why Was He Sent?

If we believe the Holy Spirit is God, then why was it necessary for Him to come? What role does He serve, and why was He sent to us? Jesus attempted to explain it to His disciples, and it is vital that we understand what He meant. If we can discover the answers to these questions, we can fulfill God's plan for our lives.

> *Most assuredly, I say to you, he who believes in Me, the works that I do he will do also; and greater works than these he will do, because I go to My Father* (John 14:12 NKJV).

One might assume that we (believers) could do more works if Jesus stayed on the earth. However, Jesus said we would do more if He returned to the Father and sent the Holy Spirit. While Jesus was on the earth, He was in a physical body and could only be in one place at a time. The Holy Spirit is not bound by location. He can be anywhere at anytime. His presence is here—right now! As Christians we have the right to His presence and have the ability to tap into God's presence through the Holy Spirit.

There is a difference between *knowing* the Holy Spirit and *having* the Holy Spirit. To know Him is to have a best friend. To have Him is to have a casual acquaintance. Do we talk to Him like a person? For instance, if a person lived in our home as a tenant, but we never talked to him, we would not really know him. God does not come to rent a room—He comes to take up residence!

Paul the apostle says:

> *But God hath revealed them unto us by His Spirit for the Spirit searcheth all things yea the deep things of God. **Now we have received**, not the spirit of the world, but **the Spirit** which is of God that we might know the things that are freely given to us of God. Which things also we speak, not in the words which man's wisdom teacheth but **the Holy Ghost teacheth** comparing spiritual things with spiritual* (1 Corinthians 2:10,12-13).

He was sent so we might know the deep things of God. When you have a deep friendship with someone, you cultivate it. The Holy Spirit is One who knows everything about the Father—what He likes, dislikes, wants, or does not want.

He comes to reveal and deepen our understanding about salvation, healing, and the love of God. There is no confusion in the Godhead. I am not belittling the Father or Jesus. It is clear from Scripture that one of the responsibilities of the Holy Spirit is to reveal Jesus (see John 14:26).

> *For you did not receive the spirit of bondage again to fear, but you have received the Spirit of adoption by whom we cry out "Abba, Father." The Spirit Himself bears witness with our spirit that we are children of God* (Romans 8:15-16 NKJV).

I am a father who enjoys blessing my children simply because I love them. I do not give them birthday or Christmas gifts because they deserve them, or because they are "well-behaved." I buy them toys, clothes, and gifts because I want to bless them.

God has paid the price for us to be blessed. He purchased us with His Son, and we receive the blessing not because we are good, but because we are His children. Some might say I spoil my children. I prefer to call it an overflowing blessing. God wants to spoil us, and He calls it prosperity. He wants to make us rich spiritually and meet all our material needs.

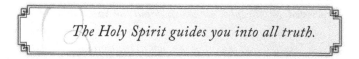

The Holy Spirit guides you into all truth.

We are heirs unto God. John 14:18 says, *"I will not leave you comfortless, I will come to you."* We are no longer orphans, we are children of God. God is our Father, and He wants to bless us. We have been adopted into God's family, and the Holy Spirit is the Agent sent to confirm the adoption:

> *For His Spirit joins with our spirit to affirm that we are God's children. And since we are His children, we are His heirs. In fact, together with Christ we are heirs of God's glory. But if we are to share His glory, we must also share His suffering* (Romans 8:16-17 NLT).

The Holy Spirit was sent to be with you, in you, and upon you!

1. *With* you:

> *And I will pray the Father, and He shall give you another comforter, that He may abide with you for ever; even the Spirit of truth; whom the world cannot receive, because it seeth Him*

not, neither knoweth Him: but ye know Him; for He dwelleth **with you...** (John 14:16-17).

He is with us to guide us into all truth, to keep us from sin, and to discover His will.

As believers, we have the Holy Spirit with us wherever we go. He will never forsake us, and abides with us. We have a destiny, and He will get us there!

2. *In* you:

*...and shall be **in you*** (John 14:17).

He is *in us* to have fellowship, communion, and to build a love relationship.

As believers, we have the Holy Spirit *in* us. He enters us to reveal His plan, personality, and purpose. We have a purpose, and He will fulfill it!

3. *Upon* You:

But ye shall receive power, after that the Holy Ghost is come **upon you:** *and ye shall be My witnesses...* (Acts 1:8).

He is *upon us* to empower us to be His witnesses, heal the sick, cast out devils, and minister to the poor.

As believers, we have the Holy Spirit *upon* us to do the works of Jesus, establish the Kingdom, and win the lost. We have a spiritual occupation, and He will complete it!

If you live your life for yourself, you will miss your destiny and purpose, and not fulfill God's plan for your life. You must not mundanely go through life, pleasuring yourself with activities (work and recreational), but instead allow the Holy Spirit to have His way in every area of your life. He will reward you beyond your dreams.

Who Is the Holy Spirit?

The following discussion is based on the information found at spirithome.com, The Holy Spirit. Christian tradition and the Bible say the Holy Spirit is equal to God.[1]

The Holy Spirit's attributes:

- Eternal – having neither a beginning, nor an end (Heb. 9:14).

- Omnipotent – having all power (Luke 1:35).

- Omnipresent – being everywhere at the same time (Ps. 139:7).

- Omniscient – understanding all matters (1 Cor. 2:10-11).

However, in a recent Barna survey, 61 percent of U.S. residents surveyed agreed with the statement that the Holy Spirit is "A symbol of God's presence or power, but is not a living entity." That belief was held by a majority (or near majority) of people in nearly every Christian denomination, including people in mainline Protestant and Evangelical churches, and was most common in non-whites and young people.

It is not a new view. Back in the days of the early church, some held that the Spirit was an "emanation" of God the Father, and others thought of the Spirit in the same terms as the Talmudic discussions on the divine Shekinah (Presence), as an expression of what Christians call the "Father."

1. The Holy Spirit Is God.

1. The Spirit's work in the Old Testament is closely identified with the word of YHWH spoken by the prophets (affirmed by the early church in Second Peter 1:21).

2. Affirmed through the close ties between Jesus' mission and the work of the Spirit (see the work of the Spirit).

3. Affirmed through the close ties between the mission of the apostles and the work of the Spirit; see First Peter 1:12.

4. Revealed during the episode with Hananiah and Ananias, when Peter declared that Hananiah lied to the Holy Spirit; and later states that he lied not to men, but to God (see Acts 5.)

5. The Trinitarian baptismal formula found in Scripture (Matt. 28:19 NKJV): *"in the name of the Father and of the Son, and of the Holy Spirit."* It dates to the church's earliest days.

2. The Holy Spirit Is a Person.

The Holy Spirit is not a symbol of an object.

- He communicates ("speaks") (see Acts 13:1-2).

- He intercedes (see Rom. 8:26).

- He testifies (see John 15:26).

- He guides (see John 16:13).

- He commands (see Acts 16:6-7).

- He appoints (see Acts 20:28).

- He leads (see Rom. 8:14).

- He reveals how wrong, foolish, or sinful a person was (see John 16:8).

- He seals God's promise in believers' hearts (see Eph. 1:13-14).

- He shapes the life of each person and community to Christ (see Rom. 8:1-17).

In Scripture, the Holy Spirit has *intellect*, *emotions*, a *will*, and can be *grieved*. This means that the Spirit has a personality (see 1 Thess. 5:19).

The key way to cause the Holy Spirit grief is through malice shown as bitterness, rage, anger, clamor (making lots of noise and disruption), and slander. Paul reveals what pleases the Holy Spirit: forgiving others as in Christ, God forgave you (see Eph. 4:32; Col. 3:13). The Spirit can act in whatever manner He chooses. He generally acts through the Church, but does not have to; the Wind blows where it will.

These qualities are not what some perceive as "The Force." Although most experience the Spirit as a Presence, this is not what the Spirit *is*. He is not a collective will or a living memory of the gathered believers, or the force of emotion, or conscience within a person. The people who teach this, fine as they may be, are describing a spirit other than the Holy Spirit. The Spirit works in all of these ways and more, yet against all of them at times. The Spirit works in whatever ways are needed to accomplish His purposes, except through forcible control of actions.[2]

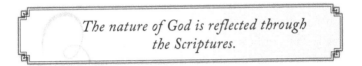

The nature of God is reflected through the Scriptures.

How do you picture the Holy Spirit? Many times, we find it difficult to look at Him as a person, because He is a Spirit. He has been described in the Bible as a dove, wind, a cloud, and breath; therefore, we find it difficult to construct an image of Him.

In Genesis 1:26, the Bible says, *"Then God said, Let us make man in **Our** image according to **Our** likeness…"* (NKJV). Notice that the word *our* is plural. It means that the reference to God is implying more than one. It is a solid indication that the Triune Godhead was involved in the creation.

The nature of God is reflected through the Scriptures. An example I have shared many times reveals *the heart of God is the Father, the face of God is Jesus, and the voice of God is the Holy Spirit.*

Matthew 10:20 says, *"For it is not ye that speaketh, but the Spirit of your Father who speaketh in you."* But the hands of God are the Church.

The Holy Spirit is *not an it*, a thing, or a *that*. When the Holy Spirit is moving in a service and the anointing is thick, afterward someone may say, "Did you feel that?!" God is not a *that*—He is a Person. What we feel is not just a presence—it is *Him*. When we sense He is standing in our midst, He is.

He did not come to glorify Himself, but to glorify Jesus.

> *Howbeit when He, the Spirit of truth, is come He will guide you into all truth for He shall not speak of Himself. ...**He shall glorify Me** [Jesus]...* (John 16:13-14).

Do not thank the Holy Spirit for what Jesus did. Thank Jesus personally and glorify King Jesus. The Holy Spirit is to be loved and worshiped, not glorified. Worship is the highest form of love, and love carries with it emotion. The Holy Spirit possesses emotions and we must be cautious not to "hurt His feelings." (Pun intended.)

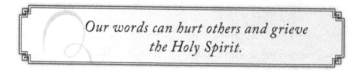

Our words can hurt others and grieve the Holy Spirit.

3. The Holy Spirit Is Sensitive.

The Holy Spirit can be easily grieved, resisted, and quenched. Sensitivity is a trait that I have observed to be more prominent in women than men. Men can be insensitive and uncomfortable when revealing their emotions. On the other hand, women tend to carry a nurturing nature that causes them to be talkative, sensitive, and emotional. It is not a negative character; rather, it is God's design.

In my opinion, I compare the sensitivity of a woman to that of the Holy Spirit. Men, however, through insensitive speech and actions toward others, can hurt their feelings, resulting in unnecessary pain, grief, and heartache that can damage relationships. Our words can cut like a knife.

> *Let no foul or polluting language, nor evil word nor unwholesome or worthless talk [ever] come out of your mouth, but only such [speech] as is good and beneficial to the spiritual progress of others, as is fitting to the need and the occasion, that it may be a blessing and give grace (God's favor) to those who hear it. And do not grieve the Holy Spirit of God, [do not offend or vex or sadden Him] by whom you were sealed (marked, branded as God's own, secured) for the day of redemption (of final deliverance through Christ from evil and the consequences of sin). Let all bitterness and indignation and wrath (passion, rage, bad temper) and resentment, (anger, animosity) and quarreling, (brawling, clamor, contention) and slander, (evil speaking, abusive or blasphemous language) be banished from you with all malice (spite, ill will) or baseness of any kind) (Ephesians 4:29-31 AMP).*

How you speak is crucial. Your words can hurt others and grieve the Holy Spirit. Do you speak abusively or aggressively to your spouse, children, coworkers? If you speak harshly, you are distressing the activity of the Spirit in your life. This opens the door to wrath, evil, and to the enemy, and grieves the Holy Spirit.

The word *grieve* means "deep sorrow" or "loss of breath."[3] In Genesis 6:6, the Bible says, *"And it repented the Lord that He had made man on the earth and it grieved Him at His heart."* When our actions offend the Holy Spirit, He takes a "deep breath," holds it, and waits for us to repent—then He can exhale His presence. When we grieve Him, He pulls back, and waits for us to change our minds and corresponding actions, so He can breathe again.

The Holy Spirit can be resisted. The Bible says, *"You stiff-necked and uncircumcised in heart and ears! You always resist the Holy Spirit; as your fathers did, so do you,"* (Acts 7:51 NKJV). We can resist the Holy Spirit in a worship service by not focusing on Jesus. The worship team attempts to lead the congregation into a higher level in the spiritual atmosphere, while we may be resisting through complaining (in our mind), "I wish they would hurry up," or "We sang this song last week," or "How many times are they going to repeat this chorus?" or "This music is too loud...do they think this is a rock concert?"

Our attitude, if unchecked, will lead us away from unity. Remember what I said in Chapter 5? God is the audience, not man. We must focus our attention on Jesus so we can experience the manifest presence of God. Embrace the worship. Praise will lift you to a new level while worship will bring you into the throne room. Come into agreement with the worship team, and then you will enter into new realms with God and engage with the King.

You do not have to wait until you get to church to experience this level of engagement. When you are in your car, take time to worship God. At home, play worship tapes or CDs. Worship music is played in my house 24 hours a day. I am creating an atmosphere for His presence, inviting angels, and prohibiting the enemy to come in by blocking His presence through praise.

If we follow this procedure, we will find it more difficult to argue with our spouse, allow tension to dominate in the home, or permit evil to reign. When worship is embraced, the Holy Spirit breathes upon us. The atmosphere is charged and changed. This is what I call "cleaning the house!" Sometimes we need our houses cleaned. We are the Temple for the Holy Spirit to indwell; and as such, we need to empty our vessels, so we can be refilled.

4. The Holy Spirit Can be Quenched.

The Bible says, *"Quench not the Spirit,"* (1 Thess. 5:19). When we participate in a worship service, there are times when we can insult the Holy Spirit. This happens when God is attempting to move, and we feel the service needs to move a different direction. At times, the praise and worship team is convinced that they must sing all five songs on their list because that is what they practiced during rehearsal. But unannounced, the Holy Spirit aggressively manifests during song number three. We may not want this, and yet, whose time are we taking? If God's presence manifests during a particular song, it means He desires to minister to the hearts of the people at that time.

Whether it is a praise or worship song, that song carries a specific meaning—deliverance, victory, healing, or intimacy—the type of song will meet a precise need for those present. After all, He is God, and knows every need. We can trust Him if He decides to change the order of the service.

Recently, at a conference our ministry was hosting, I was one of four keynote speakers. A few hours before I was scheduled to speak, my son Jordon shared some insights that the Lord had revealed to him. It was so powerful, I sensed God wanted him to share. The Holy Spirit moved and Jordon took the entire time and ministered. At the time, he was only 15. We had one of the most powerful meetings we had ever experienced. I never did speak, and I was the host speaker. God changed everything. The problem is, can we recognize when He is shifting and follow His lead? Let's be careful never to offend our Best Friend.

Best Friends

The bond between Abraham and God was so close that God called Abraham "My friend" (Isa. 41:8). Besides being an interesting concept, this concept of Abraham as a friend of God points to some fascinating and far-reaching implications. We might ask, why would God pay Abraham the great compliment of calling him His friend?

The answer can be found in comparing Abraham's relationship with God to our Christian calling. Although we may never have thought of it, Jesus Christ also views us as His friends. He said to His disciples, *"No longer do I call you servants, for a servant does not know what his master is doing; but I have called you friends, for all things that I heard of My Father I have made known to you"* (John 15:15 NKJV).

But there is more. For Jesus to call His disciples "friends" requires a pre-condition. *"You are My friends if you do whatever I command you"* (John 15:14 NKJV).

This is the key whereby Abraham came to be known as God's friend. Obedience to God was and is the prerequisite to faith and qualifying as God's friend. Paul highlighted Abraham's faithful obedience in Hebrews 11:8-10; 17-19.

I want to be God's best friend, don't you? Paul prayed, *"The grace of the Lord Jesus Christ, and the love of God, and the communion of the Holy Spirit be with you all. Amen"* (2 Cor. 13:14 NKJV).

There are seven different definitions to express communion:

1. The presence of God (making time for God).

2. Fellowship (spending personal time with God).

3. Sharing together (exchanging secrets).

4. Participation (actively involved in our lives).

5. Intimacy or intimate bond (deep affection).

6. Comradeship (with us in battle).

7. Friendship (One who never turns His back).

The Holy Spirit is a Person who talks, plans, hears, and expresses His thoughts. He is the voice of the God who leads and guides us.

His presence creates an atmosphere of comfort and safety. His Spirit is evidence of His personhood. The Holy Spirit is called holy because His nature is holy. He Himself brings a sense of reverence and glory into the very atmosphere where He is located.

He is holy, not defiled or common, but possesses all the purity and holiness of God. The dimension of His power and presence is beyond anything you will ever experience. The Holy Spirit can take an ordinary room and transform it into a holy place merely by His presence. He can take a massive arena or stadium that was designed for a sporting or secular event and transform it into the Holy of Holies. It becomes a place where God's presence resides and His manifested glory inhabits. Benny Hinn has demonstrated this both in the US and other nations.

He is so holy that if we blaspheme or speak against Him, we will not be forgiven. Matthew 12:32 says, *"Anyone who speaks a word against the Son of Man, it will be forgiven him; but whoever speaks against the Holy Spirit, it **will not be forgiven** him, either in this age or in the age to come"* (NKJV). Mark 3:29 says it this way, *"But he who blasphemes against the Holy Spirit **never** has forgiveness, but is subject to eternal con-*

demnation" (NKJV). The context of these verses reflects Jesus' reaction to the Pharisees, who attributed His ministry to the devil.

The Bible says that Jesus' ministry was the work of the Holy Spirit, *"How God anointed Jesus of Nazareth with the Holy Ghost and with power; who went about doing good, and healing all that were oppressed of the devil; for God was with Him"* (Acts 10:38). The ministry of the Church is practiced through the agency of the Holy Spirit. If a person attributes work of the Holy Spirit to the devil, it is blasphemy. It is dangerous to attribute the work of the Holy Spirit to the devil. Jesus set a demoniac free. He was busy changing lives, and the religious leaders accused Him of practicing sorcery through the means of Beelzebub. God is in the repair business, religion is in the garbage business, and satan is in the demolition business.

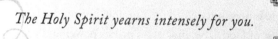

The Holy Spirit yearns intensely for you.

One of the greatest marvels the Holy Spirit does is the transformation of lives by His grace. Circumstances are changed by His mercy, and perspectives are altered by His love. This shifting comes when we yield to the Holy Spirit.

The Holy Spirit can take us beyond hearing with our natural ears and help us listen with spiritual ears—our heart. He changes our thinking, attitude, demeanor, outlook, and communication. How we speak is determined by how we think. How we think determines how we yield. The Holy Spirit is our Counselor and Guide, showing us how to take responsibility for God's work and empowering us to do it with supernatural results, giving us a place of responsibility and influence in the Kingdom.

The Spirit yearns intensely for us. We draw nigh unto Him in confident assurance and faith. *"But without faith it is impossible to please Him: for he that cometh to God must believe that He is, and that He is a rewarder of them that diligently seek Him"* (Heb. 11:6). We come nigh unto Him with unwavering faith. *"Let us draw near with a true heart in full assurance of faith, having our hearts sprinkled from an evil conscious, and our bodies washed with pure water"* (Heb. 10:22). It is imperative that we seek to draw nigh to God, having been thoroughly cleansed. You might say, "What, then, holds back my fellowship with Him and His drawing nigh to me?" Often, it is a "procrastinated surrender" of our self-directed hearts!

Michelangelo, the great Italian artist who painted the masterpiece on the ceiling of the Sistine Chapel, placed a candle in his hat while painting. He did this so that his work would never be hindered by allowing the "shadow of self" to distort the true color he desired in his painting. We need the candle of a "singleness of heart and unwavering faith," and need to work no more in the distorting shadow of ourselves. What blessed release, freedom, and liberty of spirit comes when "we" get out of the way and let the Holy Spirit have full and free access to our lives.

If you are a husband, imagine if you did not talk to your wife for days and the effect that would have on your relationship. How awkward would it be to drive in a car with someone if neither spoke for an hour? This is how God feels when we don't take the time to speak with Him. I cannot imagine not talking to Him, the Holy Spirit, frequently.

I'm constantly fellowshipping with Him whether in my prayer time, driving in my car, or working. Sometimes I express myself out loud vocally. But many times I speak to God within, on the inside of my spirit, under my breath, which works great when I am in a public place. I believe God wants us to have a constant living fellowship.

We say He is a Person, but do we converse with Him as such? Do we address Him as an individual? Benny Hinn made the phrase famous as the title of his book, *Good Morning, Holy Spirit*. If we speak to Him as if He is actually our Best Friend, dialogue will be continuous.

Can you imagine the disciples not talking to Jesus while on the earth for three years? The thought is ridiculous. *It is ridiculous not to talk to the Holy Spirit every day, because the Holy Spirit is that real.*

In First Corinthians 15, we learn that after Jesus rose from the dead, He spoke to 500 people in one setting. He told them to go to Jerusalem and wait for the Holy Spirit's arrival. They tarried in the upper room, but, interestingly, after ten days, there were only 120 present. What happened to the other 380? We may never know. But what we do know is they did not receive what the 120 did that day!

God gives the Holy Spirit to those who obey Him. If we are directed by God to go somewhere or do something, and we do not, then we forfeit the blessing that comes with obedience. Acts 5:32 says, *"And we are His witnesses of these things; and so is also the Holy Ghost, whom God hath given to them that obey Him."* People will not receive the Holy Spirit if they want to maintain control over everything in their lives. We will never experience the flow of the Holy Spirit unless we let go of *control*. This is why so many people are not filled with the Holy Spirit. The 120 were obedient to God with the singular determination that regardless of what happened, they would wait. The submission to Jesus enabled them to be in the right place at the right time.

In Acts chapter 10, the Bible introduces us to *"...a certain man named Cornelius...a devout man, and one that feared God with all his house..."* (Acts 10:1-2). Cornelius was one of the first Gentile Christians in the New Testament. Not only was he characterized as being devout and righteous, he was known by his reverence and adoration, or "fear" for the Lord. In this case, the Greek word for fear is *phobeo*, and means to show reverence, awe, or adoration toward God.[5]

Although the phrase "fear the Lord God" is common in the King James Version of the Bible, why should we fear or dread the very arms that we are lovingly drawn into with every breath? Certainly, there are some people who can only be motivated by dreadful fear, but for the rest of us, there is a far more beautiful and inspiring interpretation of these words.

Admittedly, millions have learned to have a fearful attitude, perhaps by using flawed Bible translations, or by listening to those who have blindly preached this doctrine. This unfortunate concept of fear and dread appears to be the result of the language used by Scripture translators, not from the original words of the prophets.

The word most often translated in the Old Testament as *fear* is the Hebrew word יראה (transliterated as *yirah*) that can possibly mean fear, but also means awe, reverence, respect, and devotion.[6] A closely related Hebrew word is ירא (transliterated as *yare*), which can mean fearful, but also means to stand in awe, reverence, or honor.[7]

Similarly, King James translators also chose to translate the Hebrew מורא (transliterated as *mowra*) as fear, although it also means reverence, object of reverence, or an awe-inspiring spectacle or deed.[8] Another word that King James translators chose to call fear is the Hebrew נור (transliterated as *guwr*), which can mean fear, but can also means to stir up, sojourn, dwell with, remain, dwell in, or to stand in awe.[9]

God Is a Jealous God.

Some of the newer Bible translations have translated fear with more accurate terms such as honor and reverence, to express our relationship with God. Realizing this is life-changing and alters our perceptions of God to change from an attitude of fear, and a dreadful, vengeful God, into the beautiful, loving attitude of awe, reverence, respect, and devotion toward a kind and loving God.

Compare, for example, the King James Version of Nehemiah 1:11, which reads:

> O Lord, I beseech Thee, let now Thine ear be attentive to the prayer of Thy servant, and to the prayer of Thy servants, **who desire to fear Thy name:** and prosper, I pray Thee, Thy servant this day, and grant him mercy in the sight of this man. For I was the king's cupbearer.

The New Living Translation reads:

> O Lord, please hear my prayer! Listen to the prayers of those of us **who delight in honoring You.** Please grant me success today by making the king favorable to me. Put it into his heart to be kind to me. In those days I was the king's cup-bearer (Nehemiah 1:11).

The New American Standard reads:

> O Lord, I beseech You, may Your ear be attentive to the prayer of Your servant and the prayer of Your servants **who delight to revere Your name**, and make Your servant successful today and grant him compassion before this man. Now I was the cup-bearer to the king (Nehemiah 1:11).

The New International Version reads:

*O Lord, let Your ear be attentive to the prayer of this Your servant and to the prayer of Your servants **who delight in revering Your name**. Give Your servant success today by granting him favor in the presence of this man. I was cupbearer to the king* (Nehemiah 1:11).

The fear of the Lord, as Cornelius reflects, is awe, respect, and love directed toward God. This attitude causes God to be drawn nigh unto us, attracting His presence. The Holy Spirit responds to a heart hungry for God, becoming more than a guide; He becomes our Best Friend.

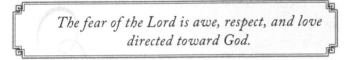

The fear of the Lord is awe, respect, and love directed toward God.

Best friends often have similarities, things in common, and parallel interests. The deeper the relationship, the more likely we are to grow close. Whatever the Holy Spirit loves, we love; whatever the Holy Spirit hates, we hate; and whatever the Holy Spirit wants, we want. The friendship increases and deepens until others might think, "They are (you and the Holy Spirit) inseparable. You never see one without the other."

Our friendship is so strong that instead of talking on the phone, text messaging someone, or emailing another, our communication is constant. We talk to Him because He is closer than a brother—He is our Best Friend. James 4:5 says, *"Do ye think that the scripture saith in vain, The spirit that dwelleth in us lusteth to envy?"* The Holy Spirit yearns with jealousy to have a love relationship with us. To yearn, in this context, means intensified longing for. He gets jealous over our time, wanting to spend time with us.

The Bible is clear—God is a jealous God. His jealousy is not based on selfishness, but upon love and is the basis for all His actions. The Holy Spirit has been sent to guide and lead us like a road map, but it is based on relationship, not just information. God is not simply our mapquest.com. He is the Person who will always be with us. When we are lonely, we are not alone. When we are discouraged, we have a Comforter. When we are hurt, we have a Friend.

How, then, do we make the Holy Spirit our Best Friend? The first thing we must do is talk to Him. When we speak, He responds. Over time, we develop the ability to hear the sound of His voice, making it easier for us to recognize His voice and develop the relationship. Solitude is necessary for intimacy; intimacy is necessary for impartation; and impartation is necessary for change. We can only change and progress with God when we have yielded ourselves to the Holy Spirit and He has complete control of our lives. Then we can call Him our Best Friend.

Endnotes

1. The portions included were taken from the spirithom.com Website; http://www.spirithome.com/spirpers.html#whois; accessed 2008.

2. http://www.spirithome.com/spirpers.html.

3. W.E. Vine, *Vine's Expository Dictionary of the Old and New Testament Words,* "Grief, Grieve," (1971), 178-179.

4. Ed Powell, "Draw Near Unto God"; http://lmi.gospelcom.net/dare. php?row=190&date=2007-07-09; accessed 2008.

5. Colin Brown, ed., *New International Dictionary of New Testament Theology* (Grand Rapids, MI: Zondervan, 1986), 619-620.

6. *Theological Wordbook of the Old Testament, Volume 1* (Chicago: Moody Press, 1980), 400.

7. Ibid.

8. Ibid., 401.

9. Ibid.

Points to Ponder

The Friendship of the Holy Spirit:

1. Who is the Holy Spirit?

_____

_____

_____

_____

2. How can you develop an intimate relationship with God through a relationship with the Holy Spirit?

_____

_____

_____

_____

9

Preparing for His Presence

Unlock the Door

GOD IS LEADING HIS BODY into a greater relationship and union with Him. The King will not allow His bride to look in any other direction but into His eyes. He will test our love and devotion. He will not have a Bride with lukewarm affections.

I believe He is preparing us by challenging our current mindsets, because we cannot fulfill His purposes with wrong mindsets or a clouded vision. The problem is, we can be clouded by our own selfish motives and lack of faith in God.

I believe there is a doorway to the presence of God. There is not a "No Entrance" sign on it, but at the same time, we cannot enter it without a key. It is as if we have only a keyhole-peeping experience through the limits of religion and unbelief knowing there must be more but settling for less. We have somehow lost the key to unlock the door that leads us to deeper relationship with God. Too often, we expect the door to His presence to open automatically.

However, we cannot enter into the secret chamber of His presence without preparation. Our preparation is the ingredient that permits our key to unlock the door to intimacy. *Fasting* is the key to unlocking the door that hinges on intimacy; once opened, we enter into God's heart, purposes, and vision.

Intimacy Restores Spiritual Visibility

There is only one thing that can restore our vision: intimacy restores spiritual visibility.

The more time we spend seeking and fellowshipping with the King, the more our perspective changes allowing us to see things from His vantage point. It is no longer our vision but becomes His vision, seeing everything through the eyes of the King. I believe the key to unlock the door to intimacy and His inner chamber is fasting.

The first extended fast I ever did, I saw results. It was one of the hardest things I ever did. I was hungry, grumpy, couldn't think, and couldn't sleep; but the deeper I got into the fast, that all began to change. I began to recognize intimacy with God and could hear Him more clearly. By fasting, spiritual clarity is created. Since then, fasting is not periodic, it has become a lifestyle. Each time I do an extended fast, I experience personal growth and an enhancement in my ministry.

One of the rewards of fasting has to do with your future. God has given you a vision, a divine dream for your life. When you fast, you open up the blessings and opportunities He has provided for you to pursue that dream. As you fast, pray for God's direction and guidance.

God impressed me to write about the importance and need to press in through prayer and fasting. To most 21st century Christians, fasting seems strange, because for nearly a century and a half, fasting has been considered a spiritual exercise to be practiced by only those thought to be "extreme" and "fanatical."

However, fasting is a necessary component for the Body of Christ to grow deeper in God and experience opportunities with the King like never before. Even though fasting has been dormant and not traditionally practiced, it is a scriptural truth (see Isa. 58:3-7). After the New Testament era, history reveals that the Church grew cold, causing the power and gifts of the Holy Spirit to become something of the past and soon forgotten.

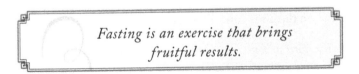

Fasting is an exercise that brings fruitful results.

Today, we are experiencing recovery of some of the lost "secrets" the early Church demonstrated on a regular basis; and we are experiencing the power that produces true biblical revival. Fasting is a God-appointed means for the flowing of His grace and power that we can't afford to neglect any longer.

Fasting is an exercise that brings fruitful results. When exercised with a pure heart and a right motive, fasting may provide a:

1. Key to unlock doors where other keys have not.

2. Window to open up new horizons of spiritual experiences.

3. Spiritual weapon from God for the struggle with sin.

What Is Fasting?

There are many misconceptions concerning fasting. Biblical fasting is not merely going without food. That's what diets are. For many, fasting is something religious monks did years ago. The practice of fasting is not just for a pastor, monk, or missionary in the past, it's for everyone, today.

Biblical fasting does include refraining from food, but for a spiritual purpose. In the natural, fasting is a purification process that cleans out the digestive system. In the Old Testament, the Hebrew people considered the bowels and the belly as the center of the body and used it to refer to the inner core of the soul.

> *The spirit of man is the candle of the Lord, searching all the* **inward parts** *of the belly* (Proverbs 20:27).

The inward parts were the location of the heart of a person.

> *But this shall be the covenant that I will make with the house of Israel; After those days, saith the Lord, I will put My law in their* **inward parts**, *and write it in their hearts; and will be their God, and they shall be My people* (Jeremiah 31:33).

In like manner, when you remove food from your diet with a purpose, your soul is cleaned from the things of the world. By flushing your soul from distractions and interruptions, your spirit becomes alert and sensitive to the Holy Spirit. Lester Sumrall said it like this, "Starve your flesh and feed your faith." We must be like David when he said:

> *As the hart panteth after the water brooks, so panteth my soul after Thee, O God. My soul thirsteth for God, for the living God: when shall I come and appear before God?* (Psalm 42:1-2).

Fasting, therefore, is the process of flushing your flesh and strengthening your spirit. Jesus said, *"...the spirit is indeed willing but the flesh is weak"* (Matt. 26:41). If we do not strengthen our spirit, we will not have spiritual power. When a father brought his son who was demonized to the disciples, they could not free the young boy from the demonic power. Jesus came upon the scene after the disciples had already prayed and commanded the demon to leave the boy. The disciples had no success.

Jesus spoke to the spirit and told it to leave him. When the disciples were alone with Christ they asked Him how he could do it when they failed. Jesus replied, *"... This kind can come forth by nothing, but by prayer and fasting"* (Mark 9:29).

Fasting is the spiritual exercise of practicing self-discipline (the denial of food, and/or things and persons) and the exercise of the heart before God in order to minister to and to glorify God. It is a spiritual exercise that should be done for God. If you need a breakthrough, clarity, or direction then fasting is a must.

When, Not If

The first observation to recognize is that if it was necessary for Jesus to fast, it must be important and significant for us as well. *"And when He had fasted forty days and forty nights, He was afterward an hungred"* (Matt. 4:2).

Second, we must recognize that God sees fasting as something He has chosen.

> *Is not this the fast that I have chosen? to loose the bands of wickedness, to undo the heavy burdens, and to let the oppressed go free, and that ye break every yoke?* (Isaiah 58:6).

Isaiah said that fasting can set captives free from wickedness, lift heavy burdens, and break every yoke. It is to be God-initiated, as if a burden is placed on us by the Holy Spirit for praying.

Jesus taught His disciples to fast. He warned about practicing our giving, praying, and fasting before others for their praise. He did not say, *"if* you fast," but *"when* you fast." He left no doubt that His disciples would obey the leading of the Spirit in this exercise.

> *Moreover when ye fast, be not, as the hypocrites, of a sad countenance: for they disfigure their faces, that they may appear unto men to fast. Verily I say unto you, They have their reward. But thou, when thou fastest, anoint thine head, and wash thy face; That thou appear not unto men to fast, but unto thy Father which is in secret: and thy Father, which seeth in secret, shall reward thee openly* (Matthew 6:16-18).

Jesus mentions fasting as a separate exercise distinct from praying. Fasting and praying are often linked in Scripture, and in experience; but they do not always have to go together. There may be times of praying without fasting, and times of fasting without unusual praying. It may not be possible to give oneself to prayer for the whole time of fasting.

Benefits of Fasting

In the Old Testament, fasting was practiced when God seemed far away. The results depended on the focus of the people. Fasting without faith and purpose is religious and will not affect or change anything.

> *Speak unto all the people of the land, and to the priests, saying, When ye fasted and mourned in the fifth and seventh month, even those seventy years, did ye at all fast unto Me, even to Me?* (Zechariah 7:5)

Fasting brings clarity and revelation. It opens the door to His presence, and when He is present, He will always speak a word in season. Many times, when I have an important decision to make, I'll do a three day fast or until I hear God speak. I believe that every decision we make can lead us closer to or lead us away from our destiny. Jeremiah 29:11 says, "*For I know the plans I have for you.*" If God has the plan for our destiny, shouldn't we spend time to seek and fast to hear the One with the plan?

That was the case in the New Testament Church when the gospel was spreading to the Gentiles. They needed direction and a plan. After fasting, God answered their prayers.

> *As they ministered to the Lord, and fasted, the Holy Ghost said, Separate me Barnabas and Saul for the work whereunto I have called them* (Acts 13:2).

We are to inquire of God whether He wants us to separate ourselves unto Him in fasting. Here are some reasons to do so:

1. For personal consecration (see Ps. 69:10; Matt. 5:4; Acts 13:3; 14:23)

2. To be heard on high (see Jer. 29:13-14; Ezra 8:23; John 4:8,31-34)

3. To change God's mind (see 2 Sam. 12:16,22; Jon. 3:5,10)

4. To free and deliver the captives (see Isa. 49:24; 58:6)

5. For revelation, understanding, wisdom (see Dan. 9:2-3,21-22; 2 Cor. 11:27; Acts 27:21-24)

6. For endowment of power, for spiritual gifts

7. To buffet the body (see 1 Cor. 9:27; 6:13-20; Rom. 13:14)

8. For physical health and healing (see 1 Sam. 30:11-15; Ps. 35:13; 3 John 2)

Through fasting, we deny the physical for the spiritual: to overcome physical drive and habits and temptations; to release us from the grip of sin; and to make our mind more alert to God.

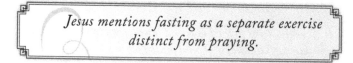

Jesus mentions fasting as a separate exercise distinct from praying.

However, a right act done with the wrong attitude is not acceptable to God. Jesus warned not to be like the Pharisees (in giving, praying, fasting) with a show of piety, self-seeking, and desiring the applause of others.

Types of Fasts

1. *Normal or regular fast* is the abstaining from all forms

of food, but not water or sleep. It can be at regular intervals, one day a week, or longer; or for a period of time at regular intervals. (See Matt. 4:2; Luke 4:2.)

2. *Absolute fast* is the abstaining from drink as well as food (usually no longer than three days). Remember, the body needs water more than it needs food. (See Acts 9:9.)

3. *Partial fast* is the restriction of diet, not to be defiled by rich food or drink (as three Hebrew children, sacrifices used to pagan gods). Many variations exist in regard to time, food, liquids, circumstances. (See Dan. 1:5; 9:3.)

How to Begin

Begin with the right motive, as God leads, and not for personal gain.

As you approach fasting, ask yourself these questions:

1. Am I confident that this desire to fast is God-given? "Jesus was led up by the Spirit to the wilderness..." (see Matt. 4:1).

2. Are my motives right? "Your Father who sees in secret will reward you" (see Matt. 6:6). You will find, as though it were Heaven's afterthought, that God who sees the heart will reward and bless openly.

3. What are my spiritual objectives in fasting? Personal consecrations? Divine guidance? Intercession? (What bur-

dens?) Fullness of spirit (for self, others)? To loose the captives? (Win souls? Release Christians?) To bring revival?

4. Are my objectives self-centered? Is my concern genuinely for others?

5. Am I determined above all else to minister to the Lord? They were worshiping the Lord and fasting.

6. Am I physically healthy enough to fast? Fasting is not always advisable, especially in cases of a person with serious undernourishment, someone who is underweight, expectant mothers, and diabetes patients using insulin.

If you have never fasted before, do not start with a forty-day fast unless you are sure that God has called you to do it. Perhaps, start with a partial fast, or a normal fast one day, no more than three. Then, you will be ready for God to call you to a longer fast. It may prove that your time of fast will be as was for Jesus, a time of conflict and struggle with satan's forces of evil.

Discouragement can come, but you can guard against it by putting on all of the full armor of God (see Eph. 6). When the going gets harder—that is wrestling, spiritual warfare—you have the weapons to win!

When my dad dealt with prostate cancer during his treatment, doctors said he received radiation burn internally. They said he would have to live with it the rest of his life and there was nothing they could do. My dad experienced severe pain for several months, was confined to bed, and couldn't work. He lost weight, was on pain killers, and had to use a catheter. Through the power of fasting and with the prayers of many, my dad was healed and fully recovered.

What Are the Results?

God gave us a pattern for release, restoration, and reward. In Matthew 6, Jesus gives us specific direction about how to live as a child of God. That pattern addresses three specific duties of a Christian: giving, praying, and fasting. Jesus says, "When you give…when you pray…when you fast." He makes it clear that fasting, like giving and praying, is a normal part of Christian life. As much attention should be given to fasting as is given to giving and to praying.

Could we be missing our greatest breakthroughs because we fail to fast? Remember the thirty, sixty, and one hundred-fold return that Jesus speaks of in Mark 4:8-20? Look at it this way: When you pray, you can release that thirty-fold return. When both prayer and giving are part of your life, I believe that releases the sixty-fold blessing. But when all three—giving, praying, and fasting—are part of your life, you can release the one hundred-fold return.

If that is the case, we have to wonder what blessings aren't being released, what answers to prayer are not getting through, and what bondages are not being broken because we fail to fast.

Jesus says fasting is the duty of every believer. When you fast, you release supernatural blessings into your life! Discover how to put this rewarding spiritual tool to work in your daily life.

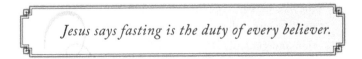

Jesus says fasting is the duty of every believer.

There are also other unexpected times when you need to capture the attention and mercy of God in your life. Fasting is the key in certain seasons and situations of your life. Consider these specific times of need for fasting.

1. *Family concerns.* When Jesus delivered the boy bound by demons in Matthew 17, He told the disciples, *"This kind does not go out except by prayer and fasting."* Maybe your kids have friends who are bad influences, maybe they are steeped in alcohol or drugs. Possibly they are struggling in school. When you don't know what else to do, pray and fast.

2. *Healing.* If you have a physical problem, fast for healing. According to Isaiah 58 when you fast, "your health will spring forth speedily."

3. *Direction from God.* Every time you face a life-changing decision, seek God's will through prayer and fasting.

4. *Financial need.* Many times the economy seems like it's on a roller coaster. If you lose your job or get behind on your mortgage payments, take it to the Lord through prayer and fasting. In Ezra 8 when Ezra faced a financial dilemma, he declared a fast and God provided the answer. He can do the same for you.

5. *Knowing your future.* God has given you a vision, a divine dream for your life. When you fast, you open up the blessings and opportunities He has provided for you to pursue that dream. As you fast, pray for God's direction and guidance. Focus your faith on your dream and God will show you how you can turn your vision into a reality. Begin pursuing your divine dream today and make the rewards of fasting part of your lifestyle.

Fasting is a principle that God intended for everyone to enjoy. It's not a punishment; it's a privilege! By making fasting a way of life, you can get closer to God and grow in your spiritual walk like never before. Fasting is one of the most powerful weapons God has given you. Through fasting, you can experience a release from the bondage of sin, restoration in your relationships, financial blessings, spiritual renewal, supernatural healing, and so much more!

Making It Happen When It Counts

*After this, the Moabites, the Ammonites, and with them the Meunites came against Jehoshaphat to battle. It was told Jehoshaphat, A great multitude has come against you from beyond the [Dead] Sea, from Edom; and behold they are in Hazazon-tamar, which is En-gedi. Then Jehoshaphat feared, and **set himself [determinedly, as his vital need] to seek the Lord; he proclaimed a fast** in all Judah* (2 Chronicles 20:1-3 AMP).*

When the King of Israel heard they were under attack, his first reaction was fear of the "ites." Fear is the first reaction when we are under attack. Like Israel, we all have some kind of "ites" in our life: job-ites, money-ites, marriage-ites, health-ites, etc.

But the king's second reaction was in response to his first, "And [he] set himself (determined, as his vital need) to seek the Lord, he proclaimed a fast in all Judah." This was the foundation of his battle strategy. His plan was to seek God with all his heart. Then he would know what to do next.

God has a battle plan for you! When you hear the news that you are under attack: work layoffs, lost retirement package, bad doctor's report, or your spouse isn't happy with you anymore, what will you do? If you follow God's plan, you will win every financial, health, or marriage battle.

Too often people try to win their battles with their own battle plan and then expect God to bless it. Jehoshaphat got very serious! He needed to hear from God. You need to hear from God. You have to be willing to turn off the television for a night and get before God. Then when you do get before God, do you know what to do next?

> *And Jehoshaphat stood in the assembly of Judah and Jerusalem in the house of the Lord before the new court and said, "O Lord, God of our fathers, are You not God in heaven? And do You not rule over all the kingdoms of the nations? In Your hand are power and might, so that none is able to withstand You. Did not You, O our God, drive out the inhabitants of this land before Your people Israel and give it forever to the descendants of Abraham Your friend?* (2 Chronicles 20:5-7 AMP)

Notice, the first thing the king did was he told God how great He was! He praises and worships God! Then he said:

> *O our God, will You not exercise judgment upon them? For we have no might to stand against this great company that is coming against us. We do not know what to do, but our eyes are upon You* (2 Chronicles 20:12 AMP).

Second, he recognized that the battle cannot be won in his strength, but in God's alone. You may feel weak in your strength, and the devil may be challenging, asking what are you going to do about it? Maybe you're facing one of the greatest battles in your life, which may involve a financial burden or you've been diagnosed with cancer.

And all Judah stood before the Lord, with their children and their wives. Then the Spirit of the Lord came upon Jahaziel son of Zechariah, the son of Benaiah, the son of Jeiel, the son of Mattaniah, a Levite of the sons of Asaph, in the midst of the assembly. He said, Hearken, all Judah, you inhabitants of Jerusalem, and you King Jehoshaphat. The Lord says this to you: Be not afraid or dismayed at this great multitude; for the battle is not yours, but God's (2 Chronicles 20:13-15 AMP).

In times of trouble, you need to take your battle positions just like the king.

And Jehoshaphat bowed his head with his face to the ground, and all Judah and the inhabitants of Jerusalem fell down before the Lord, worshiping Him (2 Chronicles 20:18 AMP).

Bowing demonstrates humility, and that your dependence and reliability is on the Lord.

During your fast, it is vital that you remain in humility. Don't make it noticeable in your mood, demeanor, or attitude that you are fasting. You don't score points with God by letting everyone know that you are sacrificing food. When you need to, dismiss yourself from others to be alone instead of sitting in the work area staring at everyone's lunch.

> *The best way to maintain humility and the proper attitude during a fast is praise.*

The best way to maintain humility and the proper attitude during a fast is praise. It prepares your heart and controls your mind. Exercise praise because it is the added ingredient to your fast that brings your victory. Praise goes before your battle.

> *When he had consulted with the people, he appointed singers to sing to the Lord and praise Him in their holy [priestly] garments as they went out before the army, saying, Give thanks to the Lord, for His mercy and loving-kindness endure forever! And when they began to sing and to praise, the Lord set ambushments against the men of Ammon, Moab, and Mount Seir who had come against Judah, and they were [self-] slaughtered* (2 Chronicles 20:21-22 AMP).

Worship confuses the enemy and always precedes a breakthrough. Notice that all the "ites" who were coming after Jehoshaphat turned against one another.

Here are seven steps to win your battle no matter what the odds:

1. Be determined to seek the Lord first.

2. Magnify the Lord, not your problem.

3. Your plans will not work without God as the source.

4. Wait on the Lord.

5. Get into position [bow in His presence].

6. Give thanks to the Lord, for His mercies endure forever!

7. Expect victory over your enemies and obstacles.

No matter who we are, we are going to face battles. The main attack from your enemy is to keep you distracted, discouraged, and disappointed in life's journey. He wants to weigh you down with burdens to prevent you from entering God's presence. Intimacy should be your goal. You need to be in His presence. Don't stop at the door. That's not far enough, go all the way.

The key to unlocking the door to His presence is fasting. When you unlock the door and walk into His presence, you will experience His glory. That is where revelation comes. Revelation brings clarity, and clarity brings peace of mind—a peace that passes understanding.

Points to Ponder

1. What is fasting?

_____

_____

_____

_____

2. What are the results of fasting?

_____

_____

_____

_____

10

Beholding His Beauty

THE JOURNEY TO *ROMANCING THE KING* is realized when we behold His beauty through pursuit of Him. We pursue God because He places an urge within us that spurs us to the pursuit. *"No man can come to Me,"* said our Lord, *"except the Father which hath sent me draw him,"* and it is by this very drawing that God removes our right for taking credit for His gracious act of kindness (see John 6:44). The impulse to pursue God originates with God, but the outworking of that impulse is our following hard after Him; while we are pursuing Him, we are already in His hand, *"Thy right hand upholdeth me"* (Ps. 63:8). In this divine "upholding" and human "following," there is no contradiction.

In practice, however, we must pursue God. On our part, there must be a positive mutual feeling if this drawing from God is to become an experience with the King.

As the hart panteth after the water brooks, so panteth my soul after Thee, O God. My soul thirsteth for God, for the living God: when shall I come and appear before God? (Psalm 42:1-2)

This is deep calling unto deep, and the longing heart will understand it.

Heart After God

David's life was a surge of spiritual desire, and his psalms ring with the cry of the seeker and the glad shout of the finder. Paul confessed the mainspring of his life to be his burning desire after Christ. "*That I may know Him*," (Phil. 3:10) was the goal of his heart, and to this he sacrificed everything.

Yea doubtless, and I count all things but loss for the excellency of the knowledge of Christ Jesus my Lord: for whom I have suffered the loss of all things, and do count them but dung, that I may win Christ (Philippians 3:8).

When Samuel anointed David to be the next king of Israel, God told Samuel:

But the Lord said unto Samuel, Look not on his countenance, or on the height of his stature; because I have refused him: for the Lord seeth not as man seeth; for man looketh on the outward appearance, but the Lord looketh on the heart (1 Samuel 16:7).

The question is, when God looked at David's heart, what did He see? We have a glimpse into what Samuel would have seen. He looked first at Eliab, the eldest son, and likely would have been culturally inclined to prefer him: first sons tended to get priority. From what

God told Samuel *not* to look at, we can assume that Samuel saw a tall, strong, handsome man, not unlike what he saw in Saul when he was anointed king over Israel.

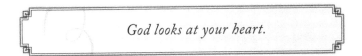

God looks at your heart.

Most of us tend to look at the outward, physical appearance when we meet a person for the first time. Some people might look for a handsome or pretty face, others for good grooming or clothing style. While these things have some value in themselves, they are obviously not what God seeks. As we get to know people, we begin to see the strength of their character and perceive their depth of integrity. Looking into someone's heart is not easy. People are nimble at putting up barriers and hiding their inner self, even from people they love.

David desired to behold God's beauty. He was a person who sought God in both the good and the bad times. His dependency upon God and his pursuit in worship, enables him to come into the presence of God. We cannot presume to look into David's heart and see what God saw. However, we do have a window, which permits us to glimpse into David's soul. That window is the psalms.

Of the 150 psalms that are recorded in the Bible, approximately half claim David as their author.[1] Many of these psalms display deep emotional responses to different situations and reveal something of the inner man. While we obviously cannot assume that everything that God saw is equally revealed in the psalms, it seems reasonable to assume that themes, which occur repeatedly and strongly in David's psalms, were likewise visible to God in David's heart.

Dependency Upon God

As we read David's psalms, two things stand out clearly: David's *dependence on God* and his *desire to worship.*

Dependency:

The Lord is my shepherd; I shall not want (Psalm 23:1).

Hear my prayer, O Lord, give ear to my supplications: in Thy faithfulness answer me, and in Thy righteousness (Psalm 143:1).

These two Scripture verses represent two of the numerous examples of David's dependence on God.

We must be careful, though, in our perceptions concerning David's dependency. It is not a "freeloading dependence," where David expected God to do everything for him, to supply all his needs promptly, and to make his life comfortable. Rather, this dependence might be called a *definitive dependence.*

David was quite capable of making decisions, taking action, and working to achieve his designed purpose. We see that clearly demonstrated in his life as a young man, as a soldier, a leader in the army, and as king of Israel. At the same time, he knew his decisions could not be trusted unless God guided them. Plans and actions would not be achievable without entrusting them to God.

There appears to be a strong contrast between the historical David, as portrayed in Samuel, and the personal David, as portrayed in Psalms.

On the one hand, we have a mighty warrior, of whom it is sung: *"Saul has slain his thousands and David his tens of thousands,"* and who commands six hundred men while in exile (see 1 Sam. 18:7; 23:13). On the other hand, we have a fearful and anxious man, who cries, *"The enemy pursues me, he crushes me to the ground, he makes me dwell in darkness like those long dead"* (Ps. 143:3).

This contrast clearly displays David's dependency on God and His provision of stability throughout his life. David certainly had enemies during his lifetime, both before he became king, when he was treated like an outlaw in his own land, and afterward, when his own son turned against him (see 2 Sam. 15). He had considerable reason to be very concerned for his life. Yet at all times he was able to command loyal followers and show genuine love for his enemies who were intent on killing him (see 1 Sam. 24; 2 Sam. 18:33).

This dependence harkens back to his youth when he was a shepherd tending his father's sheep. As he declared to Saul, before venturing out to confront Goliath:

The Lord who delivered me from the paw of the lion and the paw of the bear, He will deliver me from the hand of this Philistine... (1 Samuel 17:37 NKJV).

Even then, David had a courage that came not from knowing his own strength but from knowing his God. When God looked at David's heart on that special day, He saw David's dependency upon Him alone, and was pleased.

This dependence upon God was modeled in the life of Jesus. In the Bible, there appear numerous examples of Jesus not only claiming dependence on God, but also expressing this in prayer. This is probably best exemplified in John 5:19, where Jesus says, *"I tell you the truth, the Son can do nothing by Himself, He can do only what He sees His Father doing, because whatever the Father does the Son also does"* (NIV).

An abiding dependence on God is something that He loves to see in the hearts of His children, and something that He clearly saw in David.

Desire to Worship

The second thing that we can see in David's heart through the window of Psalms, and which Samuel would not have been expected to see, is a *heart of worship.*

Of the two themes that come through powerfully in David's psalms, I think *worship* is the strongest. The psalms, which begin with a heart-wrenching dependency, often end with uplifting worship. Worship was not simply part of his life; it was a core part of who David was.

> *I will exalt You, my God the King; I will praise Your name for ever and ever. Every day I will praise You and extol Your name for ever and ever* (Psalm 145:1-2).

A good example of these attitudes is revealed in Psalm 13, which begins, *"How long wilt thou forget me, O Lord, for ever?"* David continues to say, *"Lest mine enemy say, I have prevailed against him; and those the trouble me rejoice when I am moved,"* but ends, *"I will sing to the Lord, because He hath dealt bountifully with me."*

Psalm 63 begins, *"O God, thou art my God; early will I seek thee: my soul thirsteth for thee, my flesh longeth for thee in a dry and thirsty land, where no water is"* (Ps. 63:1). He finishes the Psalm by saying, *"But the king shall rejoice in God; every one that sweareth by Him shall glory: but the mouth of them that speak lies shall be stopped"* (Ps. 63:11).

Here he expresses both a deep need for God (with a plea that the need is not being met) and a deep faith in God, recalling all that God has done for him in the past.

David's worship is expressed in two distinct ways that are worth exploring. First, there is outward, often vocal worship: *"I will sing to the Lord,"* and *"I will extol thee, my God, O king; I will bless Thy name for ever and ever. Every day I will bless thee; and will praise Thy name for ever and ever"* (Ps. 145:1-2).

When the Ark of the Covenant was finally brought to Jerusalem, we are told that David, wearing a linen ephod, danced before the Lord with all his might (see 2 Sam. 6:14). He also sang before God, which is clearly seen from existence of the many psalms he wrote, not only in the Book of Psalms, but also in Samuel. For example, Second Samuel 22 begins *"And David spake unto the Lord the words of this song in the day that the Lord had delivered him out of the hand of all his enemies, and out of the hand of Saul"* (2 Sam. 22:1).

> *Meditating on who God is, what He has done, and what His Word says is a deeper form of worship, carrying you through the darkest times.*

Second, there is more reflective, inward worship, as expressed in Psalm 63:6-7, *"I lie awake thinking of you, meditating on you through the night. Because you are my helper, I sing for joy in the shadow of your wings"* (NLT). Many of us find it comforting to think about God during anxious, sleepless nights. To meditate on who God is, what He has done, and what His Word says is a deeper form of worship, carrying us through the darkest times. It appears David worshiped God in this manner, and God upheld him through some very dark times.

David's dependency upon God and his ability to worship in difficult times was based upon *desire!*

The Pursuit of Desire

David said, *"The one thing I have desired of the Lord is that I will seek after Him."* His passionate pursuit of the Lord was his desire.

> *One thing have I desired of the Lord, **that will I seek after**; that I may dwell in the house of the Lord all the days of my life, to behold the beauty of the Lord, and to enquire in His temple. For in the time of trouble He shall hide me in His pavilion: in the secret of His tabernacle shall He hide me; He shall set me up upon a rock. And now shall mine head be lifted up above mine enemies round about me: therefore will I offer in His tabernacle sacrifices of joy; I will sing, yea, I will sing praises unto the Lord. Hear, O Lord, when I cry with my voice: have mercy also upon me, and answer me. When Thou saidst, Seek ye My face; my heart said unto Thee, Thy face, Lord, will I seek (Psalm 27:4-8).*

We need to consider, "What is our greatest desire? What is that *one thing* our heart is longing for the most?" Is our passion and desire driving us into a deeper relationship with God, or is it driving us away from Him? What is our passion? Is our passion our occupation, sports, a hobby, cars, home, lifestyle, or even our family? Whatever consumes us, defines our passion.

David sought after God's presence and spent time in His house for all the right reasons. David was not seeking God for anything other than intimacy with Him. He dwelled in God's house to behold the beauty of the Lord, not desiring approval from others. David had a heart pursuing God.

How many times have we gone to God because we needed something? Perhaps we were in trouble and needed God's help. How would we feel if our children only came to us when they wanted something? That is selfish. Are we seeking God for all the wrong reasons?

Perhaps our rationale may be, "We're seeking God for revival." God is not seeking revival; He is seeking a Church that is longing after *Him*. Revival is a by-product of seeking Him. God sees our heart, like He saw David's heart. Too often, religion clouds our focus, and we come to God with the wrong motives.

God did not invent religion. People invented religion to keep God at a safe distance. Sometimes we substitute religion for relationship: we build a church (house) and insert Him into it. If God stays in His "house," then we can keep Him out of ours. We attend church to visit God, giving Him a Sunday of worship, while the other six days are ours.

Do we really believe that if we keep God at a "safe distance," He will not interfere with our selfish plans and desires? God is tired of duplexes where we divide the house and put Him in a room in the corner. God wants to take over the entire house!

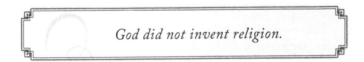

God did not invent religion.

Herein lies the problem: human traditions dictate the way we worship. However, worship is not prescribed by tradition; it stems from our heart, through His spirit. True worship is an expression of love. God does not seek our worship—He seeks *us*. He is not after our worship;

but through worship, He gets what He wants—*us!* Worship brings us into fellowship with God, so we can behold His beauty.

Where does worship begin? Worship begins with God's love. As we receive His love, we respond. When we become aware of God's love, we respond to Him with worship.

Worship is not initiated by our efforts. Worship is a response to God's love: *"**In this the love of God was manifested toward us,** that God has sent His only begotten Son into the world, that we might live through Him. In this is love, not that we loved God, but that **He loved us** and sent His Son to be the propitiation for our sins,"* (1 John 4:9-10 NKJV).

True worship is not easy to define! Worship is the only vehicle that fulfills and satisfies the longings of our hearts, and brings us face-to-face with God.

In the Old Testament, the Hebrew word for worship, *shachah*, means "to depress, to lie prostrate in homage to royalty or God."[2] In worship, one bows down or prostrates his body with his face to the ground. This posture reflects humility, surrender, and a sense of awe for the King.

> *Give unto the Lord the glory due to His name; worship the Lord in the beauty of holiness* (Psalm 29:2 NKJV).

> *All the earth shall worship You and sing praises to You; They shall sing praises to Your name. Selah* (Psalm 66:4 NKJV).

> *Oh come, let us worship and bow down; Let us kneel before the Lord our Maker* (Psalm 95:6 NKJV).

> *…Come up here and I will show you things…* (Revelation 4:1 NKJV).

The highest priority of worship is that God invites us into His presence—*not* that we selfishly invite Him into ours. The value of our worship is determined by the sincerity of the worshiper, which takes priority over the method and ability of *how* we worship.

In the New Testament, the word *worship* is the Greek word "proskuneo," which means to kiss. We talked about "kissing God with worship" in Chapter 5. The Greek concept is to bow before one's feet and lean forward in a token of reverence.

God Wants *Intimacy!*

True worship eliminates the distance between God and us. Many believers avoid true worship because it brings them face to face with God, and they do not want to face Him because they have not faced themselves. We cannot *behold His beauty* with unconfessed sin in our lives.

> *And we, who with unveiled faces all reflect the Lord's glory, are being transformed into His likeness with ever-increasing glory, which comes from the Lord, who is the Spirit* (2 Corinthians 3:18 NIV).

In holy *intimacy*, the veil that once covered our faces is removed. Worshipers come face to face with God, and are transformed into His likeness. God does not want to touch us merely with His presence; He wants us to stay with Him.

Meet Him on the Mountain

To behold His beauty, we must meet with Him on the mountain. In ancient times, the meaning of the mountain was significant. Heathen high places were frequently erected on open hilltops (see Deut. 12:2). It was commonly believed that the higher the elevation, the closer they were to the gods. The God of Israel used this contemporary belief and called His people to the mountain.

> *Then the Lord said to Moses, "Come up to me on the mountain…* (Exodus 24:12 NIV).

The frequent references to mountains and hills are both literal and figurative. God calls the entire land of Israel "My mountains" (see Isa. 14:25; 65:9). Mountains were often chosen as the place for worship, or a place for a divine revelation: Sinai (see Exod. 19:18-20), Moriah (see Gen. 22:2), Zion (see Ps. 2:6), and Carmel (see 1 Kings 18:19-39).

Mountains are a place to extend one's vision (see Deut. 3:27). They influence rainfall and are related to productivity (see Ps. 29:3-9); they are symbols of permanence (see Hab. 3:6) and stability (see Ps. 30:7); and are personified to give expression to human emotions— shuddering judgment (see Ps. 18:7) and rejoicing at the event of Israel's redemption (see Ps. 98:8; Isa. 44:23; 49:13).

It makes sense, then, why Jesus was transfigured on the mountain. This experience clearly defines this chapter, Beholding His Beauty.

> *And after six days Jesus taketh Peter, James, and John his brother, and bringeth them up into an high mountain apart, and was transfigured before them: and His face did shine as the sun, and His raiment was white as the light. And, behold, there appeared unto them Moses and Elias talking with Him. Then answered Peter, and said unto Jesus, Lord, it is good for us to be here: if Thou wilt, let us make here three tabernacles; one for Thee, and one for Moses, and one for Elias. While he yet spake, behold, a bright cloud overshadowed them: and behold a voice*

out of the cloud, which said, This is My beloved Son, in whom I
am well pleased; hear ye Him. And when the disciples heard it,
they fell on their face, and were sore afraid. And Jesus came and
touched them, and said, Arise, and be not afraid. And when
they had lifted up their eyes, they saw no man, save Jesus only
(Matthew 17:1-8).

The word *transfigured* is a very interesting word. The Greek word
is "metamorpho" and it means to transform (literally or figuratively),
to "metamorphose," or to change.[3]

The word is a verb, which means to change into another form. It
is also defined as to change the outside to match the inside. The prefix
"meta" means to change and the "morphe" means form. In the case of
the transfiguration of Jesus Christ, it means to match the outside with
the reality of the inside, changing the outward so that it matches the
inward reality. Jesus' divine nature was "veiled" (Heb. 10:20) in human
form, and the transfiguration was a glimpse of that glory. Therefore,
the transfiguration of Jesus Christ displayed the shekinah glory of God,
incarnate in the Son. The voice of God attesting to the truth of Jesus'
sonship was the second time God's voice was heard. The first time was
at Jesus' baptism into His public ministry by John the Baptist (see
Matt. 3:7; Mark 1:11; Luke 3:22).

In this context of confusion among the disciples, we read the
transfiguration story. Six days went by after Peter's confrontation with
Jesus, apparently uneventful but no doubt filled with confusion on the
part of the disciples. Jesus took Peter, James, and John up "to a high
mountain" where they witnessed a most wonderful sight. Jesus was
glorified before their eyes. His body took on a different appearance (see
Matt. 17:2). Moses and Elijah appeared. When we think about it, these
two characters fit perfectly in this scene. Moses was the great lawgiver

in Israelite history, but he was also the first of God's great prophets (see Deut 18:14). Elijah was also a great prophet of God.

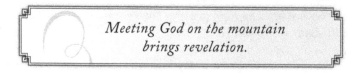

Meeting God on the mountain brings revelation.

Furthermore, both of them experienced an appearance of God: Moses in Exodus 33:17, and Elijah in First Kings 19:9, with both appearances occurring on mountains, Mount Sinai and Mount Carmel.

Like Jesus, both men had performed mighty works in the name of the Lord God of Israel and had experienced, to some degree, the rejection of their own people. In addition, these two characters have symbolic significance, as well. Together they represent the Law and the prophets, both of which point to Jesus (see Rom. 3:21). But now the focus was to be upon Jesus.

The transfiguration of Jesus sets the tone for the focus of this chapter, Beholding His Beauty. On the transfiguration mount, the dramatic change in Jesus' appearance occurred when He was praying and communing with God. To a lesser degree, the countenance of Moses had also changed when he had been in the presence of God (see Exod. 34:29-30). What is on the inside shows on the outside, as when Stephen, the first Christian martyr, was testifying to the truth—his face shining like that of an angel (see Acts 6:15).

As Jesus was praying in this glorious state, Moses and Elijah appeared in visible form, talking with Jesus about His soon coming departure that He would accomplish in Jerusalem (see Luke 9:31). God the Father had revealed what would happen to Jesus. The prophets' words were certainly meant to strengthen Jesus for the trials and suffering He willingly was soon to endure.

Peter was so excited to behold these "great men of old" that He inappropriately suggested constructing three tents, one for each of them, so they could stay longer and, undoubtedly, provide Peter the opportunity to speak with them. Peter may have assumed that this was the beginning of the Messiah's earthly reign as King, but this was not God's timing.

God interrupted Peter by causing a bright, thick cloud to cover Jesus, Moses, and Elijah, and spoke profound words, similar to the words He spoke at Jesus' baptism, *"This is My beloved Son in whom I am well pleased. Hear Him!"* (Matt. 17:5 NKJV). God desires that we listen to and obey Jesus, for He is far greater than Moses, the great lawgiver, or Elijah, the great prophet. God wanted Peter to know that he could not put His Son on the same level of importance as Moses or Elijah. God wants us to grasp the importance of hearing the Word of the Lord, not just seeing wonderful sights or having great experiences; what is more important is hearing the Word of the Lord. God emphatically commanded that we listen to Jesus!

How Does This Apply to Us?[4]

First, it reveals *who Jesus is*. The disciples, Peter speaking on their behalf, had confessed that Jesus was the Messiah. But they had a mistaken idea of what Messiah meant, and Jesus' depiction of His pending death had confused them. The transfiguration confirmed Peter's confession, revealing to Peter, James, and John that Jesus was no ordinary man, nor even a great prophet, but that He was the Son of God, the Messiah of Israel.

Meeting on the mountain brings a revelation of who Jesus is. In His presence, we discover the meaning of God's Son. One minute on the mountain transforms us into the character of Christ, where we will be metamorphosed into His nature. When we come face to face with God, like Moses, we cannot walk away from the experience and remain the same. We will be changed, reflecting the Son!

Second, this scene *gives affirmation from the Father*. A voice from Heaven resounded to earth, saying, *"This is my beloved Son"* (Luke 9:35). After we discover who Jesus is, then we can understand who we are. When we are in His presence, beholding His beauty, we discover our purpose. We gain our identity, are affirmed, and are welcomed into the arms of Abba, our Daddy!

We take the place of Moses and Elijah. The Holy Spirit ushers us into the presence of glory where the Father invites us, while we celebrate Jesus. This is the meaning behind *Romancing the King*.

Third, the transfiguration confirms that in the presence of the King, there is glory. In the transfiguration, Peter, James, and John saw a foretaste of the glory. In the transfiguration, we see the King of righteousness in His glory; we see the glory of His person, His Kingdom, and His nature.

The transfiguration is a glorious revelation and a glorious experience for both Jesus and the three disciples to witness. Through their anticipation of His death and resurrection, we can anticipate His arrival—not just at the end of the age, but now. The Kingdom of God is here! We get to experience the glory of the resurrection. We are permitted to come to the mountain and fellowship with the King of kings.

Fourth, the scene was to demonstrate the purpose and destiny of our lives when in God's presence. The discussion between Moses and

Elijah was the *departure* of Jesus. The King James Version translates it "decease." The Greek word is *ex-odos,* also known as exodus. "Ex" means exit or out. The word *odos* means pathway or journey. Combined, *exodus* means the pathway out.

The purpose of Jesus was to come and redeem humanity, and His destiny was the cross and resurrection. On the mountain, we discover our purpose. The Bible says, *"For I know the thoughts that I think toward you, saith the Lord, thoughts of peace and not of evil, to give you an expected end,"* (Jer. 29:11). God's plan for our lives is revealed on our Mount of Transfiguration. Our destiny is revealed when we meet Him face to face. The transfiguration of Jesus Christ is a unique display of His divine character, and a glimpse of the glory that Jesus had before He came to earth in human form. This truth is emphasized for us in a passage in the apostle Paul's letter to Philippi.

> *Let this mind be in you, which was also in Christ Jesus: Who, being in the form* [morphe] *of God, thought it not robbery to be equal with God: But made Himself of no reputation, and took upon Him the form* [morphe] *of a servant, and was made in the likeness of men: And being found in fashion as a man, He humbled Himself, and became obedient unto death, even the death of the cross. Wherefore God also hath highly exalted Him, and given Him a name which is above every name: that at the name of Jesus every knee should bow, of things in heaven, and things in earth, and things under the earth; and that every tongue should confess that Jesus Christ is Lord, to the glory of God the Father* (Philippians 2:5-11).

It is in the deepest form of worship that we meet Him on the mountain, and reverence His lordship. The cry to worship has been proclaimed, and we must respond to His call. The Holy Spirit is leading the saints to a new level: it is time to worship! Our hunger for Him will define our pursuit as we fall in love—in love with our Lord, all over again.

We must experience intimacy with God by *Romancing the King!*

Endnotes

1. Gordon D. Fee and Douglas Stuart, *How to Read the Bible for All It's Worth* (second edition) (Grand Rapids, MI: Zondervan Publishing House, 1993), 193.

2. Charles F. Pfeiffer, Howard F. Vos, John Rea, eds, *Wycliffe Bible Dictionary* (Peabody, MA: Hendrickson Publishing, 1998), 1823.

3. *Wycliffe Bible Dictionary,* 1731.

4. The content in this section was based on the Expository Files 4.11, Understanding the Transfiguration, by David McClister, Nov. 1997.

Points to Ponder

1. What is the pursuit of desire when it comes to worship?

_____

_____

_____

_____

2. How can you be transformed to a new level in God and experience the deepest relationship with your King?

_____

_____

_____

_____

More About the Author

*For information about Brian Lake Ministry conferences
or to order more books, contact:*

Brian Lake Ministries
PO Box 305
11860 Great Cove Rd.
Needmore, PA 17238

Call: 717-573-4040

Visit: www.brianlake.org

Email: info@brianlake.org

Other books from Brian Lake Ministries

Designed to Dream

The Fire Within

The Fragrance of Healing

———○———

In her book *Designed to Dream*, Pamela Lake shares how to discover your dream or destiny. God's master plan includes everyone. Each person is created with many things in common that connect us with our surroundings. Yet each person is distinct from all other human beings.

———○———

Get ready for a fresh touch from Heaven in Jordan Lake's first book, *The Fire Within*.

It only takes a spark to get a fire burning, and if the weather conditions are just right, a small fire can consume a large portion of land in a matter of days. That is how it is with God. The power of God can stir intense heat and become a consuming fire. The fire of God motivates us to action. We are more productive for God when there is a fire within. A blaze of glory creates a deep passion for souls and a desire to serve people.

———○———

Molly Lake shares how believers can smell the aroma of the anointing in her first book, *The Fragrance of Healing*.

Molly describes how to enter into a deeper relationship with God through worship, sacrifice, and service. *The Fragrance of Healing* brings a spiritual anointing into your heart and spirit that becomes a pleasing aroma to God.